# Dyke Delusions

Essays & Observations

by
Samantha Mann

Published by

Read
Furiously

Published by Read Furiously. First Edition - Trenton, NJ.

ISBN: 978-1-960869-16-6
LCCN: 2025933672

Memoir
Essays
LGTBQIA+
Women Authors
Modern/21st Century

Portions of this book have been previously published online or in print in other publications. Please conslult the Permissions section for a full list of these credits.

For more information on *Dyke Delusions* or Read Furiously, please visit readfuriously.com. For inquiries, please contact info@readfuriously.com.

Read (v): The act of interpreting and understanding the written word.

Furiously (adv): To engage in an activity with passion and excitement.

**Read Often. Read Well.**
**Read Furiously**

# About Dyke Delusions

*Dyke Delusions: Essays and Observations* is a nonlinear memoir that reclaims the notion of self as it reminds us to sit with the discomfort that comes with the journey. In a mix of personal essays and cultural criticism, Samantha Mann confronts body politics, motherhood, queerness, sexuality, and childhood trauma in a way we haven't seen before. Published work and never-before-seen essays come together for fans who were eagerly waiting for the follow-up to Mann's first book of essays, *Putting Out: Essays on Otherness*.

Samantha Mann opens her collection with a close reading of the word "dyke," from her personal history with the word to the reclamation that ends with hope and possibility. From there, the ebb and flow of writing matches the healing waters that Mann searches for in "Good and Clean and Fine," by stating clearly, "We're meant for bigger things." *Dyke Delusions* explores the liminal space between childhood and adulthood, whether it's Mann understanding her queerness as a camp counselor in "Camp Out" or finally finding love and living the life she deserves in "Great Escape."

Told in Samantha Mann's pitch-perfect observations and signature humor, *Dyke Delusions* is a collection filled with desire, yearning, and a search for more. Every essay connects to something bigger than us - emphasizing the importance of being honest with ourselves and with each other. The message behind *Dyke Delusions* is essential: we need to be talking more.

To Oliver and Sylvie, may you always stay true to your most authentic selves, but in the likely case that you don't, remember you can always find your way home.

The great revelation perhaps never did come. Instead there were little daily miracles, matches struck unexpectedly in the dark; here was one.

~Virginia Woolf , *To The Lighthouse*

# Contents

# How Horny Are Moms?

# Part IV (Womanhood)

# Author's Note:
## On Dykes: Reclaiming and Solace

I knew of dykes before I had language to describe them. Unlike many people I spoke with regarding the topic, my first introduction to dykes was wholly positive and sealed off from any negative cultural impact.

At the tender age of eleven, at my Girl Scout summer camp, I was introduced to a new type of woman. This was around 1999-2000, so it's possible that today many of these people use they/them pronouns or are transgender, but varying identities and gender expressions were not as open as they are today. All the counselors I knew used she/her pronouns. The counselors in charge of us were college-aged, or slightly older for those attempting to hold on a little longer to carefree summers removed from the real world. Of course, there were generic appearing women, gender-conforming, mainstream looking coeds, but there was a large population of *other* women, who I would later learn fit the term "dyke."

None of them talked to us about their sexuality (until we were teenage campers and we begged them for details about their personal lives), so more than an association with dating or sex, I learned about the various ways a "woman" could be. Many of them wore their hair violently short, some fully buzzed. Their broad shoulders and muscly arms stood out as they swaggered across the campgrounds. Dressed in tank tops, board shorts, with literal carabiners hooked onto their belt loops and backward baseball hats or tied bandanas, they were the embodiment of tomboys. The dyke counselor ranged from hard butch to the softer chapstick variety, from vegans to carnivores, and from animal rescuers to climate activists. They were all feminists. One particular dyke counselor I had adorned her ears with rainbow studs that started at her lobe and reached the top of her helix. Her platinum curls are always in pigtails. After a three day hike on the Appalachian Trail, we stopped off at a Taco Bell where she accidently ingested a few bites of a meat taco and then proceeded to cry for the remaining hour ride back to the camp. I wished I cared about anything as much as she cared about the wellbeing of animals. At fireside jam sessions the dykes belted The Cranberries, Sheryl Crow, and Madonna. Their laughter howled, booming through the campsite. Their farts and burps bellowed. They encouraged us to climb and dig and play with fire. The dykes were unladylike in the most intoxicating way. It was beautiful to bask amongst them.

The dykes provided bear hugs before bed if we felt homesick, and taught us how to play rugby. Contrary to other adult women in our lives, the dykes never commented that we were pretty or asked us about boyfriends. They told us we were brave, tough, and kind. At archery practice, I watched a girl twist her ankle and fall to the ground crying. Out of nowhere, a dyke counselor sprinted across the field, lifted her, and ran her to the nurses' station faster than the golf cart could drive down to meet us. Never in my life had I felt safer than being around the dykes. I wonder if the brashness and confidence they exuded followed them outside the refuge of our forest. Camp Kittamaqund was located in the quaint town of Burgess, Virginia, and although it was a city known for deeply conservative values, the few miles of camp acted as a sacred place for us all. I wanted to be near them. I wanted to be friends with them. Even though I preferred more feminine clothing and ways of presenting, I felt a kinship that in my youth I couldn't articulate. I wanted to grow up and live like then. Exactly the way I pleased. Fearless.

The mainstream boogeyman words associated with dykes - scary, ugly, violent, dirty feminists - never crossed my mind. But, sometime between middle school and high school, near the end of my camp career, these negative stereotypes seeped into my psyche. During the time between 2002-2006, I was a high school student and didn't see varied or positive representations of queer women anywhere, except for *The L Word*, which seemed more like a fictional galaxy than a sliver of real life. We all witnessed the tragedy of Ellen DeGeneres's attempt to gracefully come out of the closet in 1997. The moment acted as a warning for many. While her daily talk show *The Ellen Show* was a hit during this time, the fear and sting of the public not initially welcoming her lingered. We saw her transform into what I consider an easily digestible lesbian: perky, nonthreatening, asexual, obsessed with giving away free stuff to middle-aged moms. Throughout the early 2000's gay men were having more of a positive mainstream cultural movement: *Will and Grace*, *Angels in America*, *RuPaul's Drag Race*, and the famous coming outs - Ricky Martin, Lance Bass, and Neil Patrick Harris, to name a few. Lesbian women were not finding the same open arms. In 2010 mega star country singer Chely Wright came out of the closet and watched as her entire career imploded. Radio stations banned her music. Death threats and letters condemning her to hell followed. By the time I reached high school I internalized the word "dyke" as a slur, and most importantly it was *the* insult you didn't want hurled at you.

The summer between 9th and 10th grade was my last at summer camp, and I went in with a clearer picture of the dykes. Now I knew some of them had been whispered about, bullied, or worse in their schools and towns. At sixteen I knew "tomboy" was a phase you were supposed to have outgrown. Mostly, I knew it was easier to keep your head down and blend in. The dykes did not adhere to any of this obvious knowledge. I entered my last camp summer as an almost-adult feeling bold enough to press a particular counselor about what it was like to be with another woman (No doubt she could sense my sapphic inclinations). She bestowed mere morsels: *amazing, soft, otherworldly*. In the woods, I couldn't wait to get to college and start kissing girls, but having the fuller picture of the social and cultural implications of being an out dyke made it feel like a confusing secret. Under the protection of oversized pines and oaks, I felt proud to be associated with the dykes, but I knew this was an artificial wonderland. It would have been easier to have stayed in the woods. I wondered what my counselors faced outside the safety of the natural greenery, but I didn't ask. I didn't want to know. I needed to maintain them as superheroes.

I don't remember exactly the first time I heard "dyke." I

assume I first heard it as a slur. By junior year of high school, I knew "dyke" was the worst thing you could call another girl - worse than "slut," "whore," or even "fat" (which came in a close second in 2004). "Dyke" was a word to indicate a person was subhuman- certainly sub-girl. It was reserved for the biggest outcasts. In high school, I primarily heard it by girls against girls. When the word fluttered around me, I'd freeze, holding my breath like the word was a drug sniffing dog who might discover me. When I could, I'd force out a squeaky laugh of approval. The word was mostly reserved for tomboys, which left me safe as a gender-typical high schooler. (I did go through a phase senior year where I wore baggy jeans and oversized band T-shirts, but the shirts belonged to my boyfriend and I was taking Xanax during the day, so I chalked it up to that and no one bothered me about it.). Although I escaped having the word aimed at me for the entire four years, a change occurred, and I mentally turned my back on dykes. By graduation I wondered why lesbians couldn't all be girly. Did they really need to be boy-ish and call all that attention to themselves? I was terrified of butch women. And, of course, secretly turned on by them.

I left for college ready to explore my sexuality equipped only with one secret lesbian date and the first four seasons of *The L Word*. While I was anxious to practice drunk-kissing my friends, I stayed on high alert knowing that the word "dyke" was to be avoided and eradicated. I didn't even like "lesbian." I thought it sounded like an STI. More than anything, I left for college with the hope that I was a blossoming bisexual who happened to have never felt a twinge of romantic connection with any boy she'd ever met.

By spring semester freshman year, I enrolled in Gender and Sexuality Studies 101 and had spent the last five months drunk-kissing girls. An energy I'd never experienced, like being struck by lightning and gaining superpowers instead of dying, radiated through me that spring. Sitting in American History the morning after I felt a girl up for the first time (the experience was awkward and wonderful- I remember being surprised to feel volume where flatness usually lay), I finally understood what people meant when they said they could die happy. I met a dyke in my gender studies class and once a week secretly went to lunch with her. She would invite me to rugby team parties or suggest we study together over the weekend, but I declined, making up one dull excuse after another. The impulse to present as preppy, and pretty, and join a sorority with my friends pulled at me. At my traditional Southern school I couldn't be associated with dykes. While I was flying high from exploring authentic parts of myself, I didn't sign up for Gender and Sexuality Studies 102 (which I still regret) and I never asked my new friend out on a date, despite wanting to. Although it was harder to stop kissing girls.

The first time I was called a "dyke," it happened behind my back. There were rumors swirling through the sorority houses about me and particularly about my best friend (my now wife LOL). She endured more gossip due to her obvious lack of interest in dating. She hardly spoke to guys, and certainly was never seen touching them. Every now and then she made an effort to lie about her past experiences and crushes, but lying didn't come as naturally to her. Luckily for me, I was deep into exploring all aspects of my sexuality.

It helped that sleeping around garnered positive social attention. Most weekends I was seen sloppily making out with a frat guy, leaving someone's apartment, or engaging in an early morning walk of shame. At a Sunday night potluck, a sorority Barbie posed a question to the group: "who let those dykes in here?" When a friend told me about this, reassuringly that *of course I wasn't a lesbian, LOL, RIGHT?* It felt like I had been stomped in the chest with one of their high heels. A year later, someone I considered a good friend texted me just to tell me I was a "stupid dyke." To this day, no one has called me a dyke to my face in a derogatory way. In many ways, I've been lucky.

After I crawled out of the closet at 22, I continued to maintain my distance from the word. I internalized dyke as a slur and didn't want to be associated with it. Even after a handful of out years and becoming more comfortable with myself, I kept the word at arm's length.

Approximately four months into the pandemic and a decade after coming out of the closet, I experienced an internal tectonic shift. Maybe this was spurred by living in Brooklyn during the summer of 2020 - being surrounded by marches, protests, standing on my balcony with a baby on my hip banging pots and pans every night at 7 PM, cooking meals for our local food bank, and observing community in action for the first time, all while feeling the world could be coming to end - but I unearthed a rooted sense of self. During the early pandemic months, I began eating three full meals a day and snacking when I wanted. This was an extraordinary change from my prior life of snacking lightly throughout the day and eating a light dinner all while feeling self-congratulatory for sustaining sensations of hunger. Over the summer of 2020, I started buying the beloved junk food from my childhood at our bodega every night for dessert: zebra cakes, hostess cupcakes, moon pies, and Snickers ice cream bars. Until that summer, I'd never routinely eaten dessert. I gained some weight, but for the first time it didn't feel like a crisis. Like the rest of the world, I was relishing any comfort I could latch onto. Somewhere between the late night desserts and discovering a sense of body neutrality, I started referring to myself as a dyke. Maybe it was seeing old ways of being thrown out the window, or more likely witnessing how broken and problematic they were. In an upside world, the word "dyke" felt like a comfort.

In the spring of 2021, I had the immense privilege and absolute pleasure of interviewing American photographer J.E.B about her grounding and first of its kind anthology, *Eye to Eye: Portraits of Lesbians* for BUST's digital magazine. The interview, which was a speed class on the outlaw life of lesbians in our country during the 1960s and 1970s filled me with an immense sense of pride and connection. At the end of the interview, I confided to J.E.B about the nagging guilt I carried for being legally married and having a child who, despite not being biologically mine, had my name on his birth certificate. Over Zoom we both started crying and she assured me there was nothing to feel guilty about (actually, she told me feeling guilty was stupid and useless), and that the only antidote was to do one positive thing for someone else every day. J.E.B exuded everything I internally knew to be true about dykes: bravery, a community builder, kindness, humor, and eternally hopeful.

How could I not want to be associated with such a person and word?

When I went looking for an examination on the word "dyke," mainly how queer women personally relate to it, I discovered that there is almost nothing, which seems wild for a word so evocative. I expected to find Sontag's *On Dykes* only to learn that she remained "quasi-closeted" and didn't speak much to her sexuality. Alison Bechdel's weekly comic strip, *Dykes to Watch Out For*, which ran from 1983-2008, showed the complexity and a varied representation of lesbians. While the word "*Dyke*" is used in the title and implies the inclusiveness of the community, it continues to be a divisive word not fully embraced by the community. In 2014 writer Natalie Dicou wrote an essay in the Atlantic titled, "How I Learned to Stop Worrying and Love Being a 'Super Dyke'" where she details her transitions from fearing to embracing the word.[1]

Additionally, Olivia Mills, a student at American University, wrote a paper in 2022, "What's In A Word: The Disaccord on Dykes" In the paper, Mills points out not only her own personal discomfort with the word, and how this translates to our community being uncomfortable, anxious, and disjointed regarding the word.

In the paper, Mills quotes author and activist Julia Penelope, (June 19, 1941 – January 19, 2013) an American linguist, author, philosopher, and self-described "white, working-class, fat butch dyke who never passed," as saying, "But here we are glibly talking about 'reclaiming our past' when many of us aren't even dead yet! *Whose* past are we 'reclaiming?'" Mills agrees somewhat, but adds her own thoughts, "How do you reclaim a word that has over a century-long history of homophobia and misogyny? How do you say it proudly without thinking of all the pain that your community has endured? For some, that history and great weight is what gives them power and the confidence to own this complicated word."[2] I tend to agree with Mills in believing that by taking on the complication and great weight of the word "dyke" as our own, we alter and shift its negative meanings. I imagine each person who recovers the word for themselves rinsing off bits of the hate, leaving less and less behind until we've collectively transformed *dyke* into a neutral descriptor or maybe even one of admiration.

Desperate to know what queer women thought in the early days of 2024, I took to Instagram to take the temperature on the term. In a simple insta-story I prompted the question: "Queer Women - what is your relationship to the word *dyke*?" Abou 40 people responded, messaging a handful of words to multi-paragraphs. Overall, it seemed that the majority of women were thrilled to refer to themselves as a "dyke" citing it as an act of reclamation. It should be noted that most of the women who responded to my call for information about their relationship on the word "dyke" were white, between their late 20's to early 40s, and active online. These characteristics could contribute to their level of comfort and overall usage of the word.

In the group of pro-dyke identifiers, I summarized and categorized their overall thoughts:

- I love this! It is my preferred way of self-identifying.
- I love this! I feel powerful after reclaiming it from

an experience when it was used against me in a negative, violent way.
- I love it but hate it when the straights use it.
- I love it, and this piece of art helped me embrace it (AB's *Dykes to Watch Out For*, JEB's *Eye to Eye*, Catherine Opie's image *Dyke*, Jenny Fran Davis's novel, *Dykette*)

A second category of responders had similar swaths of ideas:
- I like the word, but I don't feel like I can use it because I'm not butch enough, not masc. enough, "cool" enough, edgy enough, or another thought of not fitting a certain mold here, and I don't like people's reaction when I say it.

The third group of responders (which was smallest) noted:
- I do not like this word. It has a harmful history and I don't want to perpetuate it.

The overarching theme for those that like the word, but don't use it is that they don't feel like it's for them in some way. In this genre, a handful of black queer women also reported that it felt like a word used more for white queer women. No follow up on this idea was reported.[3]

Overall, it was revealed that many queer women feel gatekept from the word, primarily as it is related to gender presentation. The great thing is there is no historical hard line on the word. It is the most inclusive word we have. Dyke doesn't correlate to gender presentation, sexual preferences in the bedroom, race, ethnicity, generation, or one's stance on how many floral tattoos is considered too many. There is no wrong way to dyke.

This collection, *Dyke Delusions*, is an attempt to expand from reclaiming *dyke* to reconsidering other parts of myself that I was taught to internalize with shame and rigid rules. This essay collection has been organized in the vein of embracing the nonlinear process which mirrors my relationship to healing from various traumas. The nonlinear framework had been presented to me numerous times throughout my seemingly endless therapeutic work and yet it was an idea I wrestled against as I craved a clear-cut route. In the past, I've viewed setbacks as pitfalls and steps forwards as leaps. Always to be left feelings miles away from my goal of completed healing. Now I realize my original notions of being completely healed were fixed in the hopes of fully forgetting. Eventually, I gave up on this concrete and nonsensical sentiment and leaned into the truth: healing is a long and winding road that often leaves one carsick. If you choose to read the essays straight through, which isn't required, you may find yourself asking, is she going backward in time? Is she going forward in time? Did I already read about that event? Is she changing between present and past tense? Is she contradicting an early experience or emotion or experience? The answer to all of this is yes. Moreover, the collection struggles to reexamine prior labels I used to avoid, and perhaps find solace in them too. It hopes to question: exactly who, or what, is delusional here? For a long time, many of us believed we were the crazy ones.

It's clear now: I always knew dykes were beautiful and powerful. It wasn't until I was knee-deep in cultural bullshit that I felt scared and confused of the word, and ultimately myself. I have always had an ingrained, natural knowing of what is right for me. My intuition and guts have always been the best system I have for finding myself, my people, and my path. I lost this ability by the time I hit my early teen years due to pop culture, family structure, community culture, etc. and have since spent my adulthood relearning how to listen to my truth without the external noise. This path is true for many of us, especially those with marginalized identities. Now I find comfort in "dyke," how it conjures the scent of evergreens, the sensation of the warming sun on my skin, provides a boost of grit, and connects me to a legacy of community builders and activists. It acts as an important connector to the past and the ability to carry us together into the future. I implore you, if you want it, then *dyke* is for you.

# Part I:
## Body Work

# Dismantle

In a tired, thick album inside my parents' overstuffed hall closet sit a couple of photos, telling the origin story of my joy for self-exposure. When I examine the photos, I can't tell if I remember the moment or if I have created an inauthentic memory from a lifetime's worth of my family's storytelling. In the pictures I wear a short white skirt with a bubble gum pink T-shirt. All the cotton articles appear baggy denoting a sign of the times. My young bare feet point as I am captured mid-dance. Perfectly cut chestnut bangs line my forehead and my ponytail swings as I stand forever frozen in a twirl. On a ferry lined with dingy crimson carpet and shellacked wooden benches, I put on a show.

You can't see my mom or granny in the photos. Just me and a crowd of strangers.

Specifically, as my mom tells it, the three of us were taking a ferry to Chincoteague Island for a daytrip during our beach vacation in South Carolina. Suburban legend has it that halfway across the bay the crew started blasting music through the loudspeakers and right away I bounced off my mom's lap and started dancing. I danced up such a storm grown folks gravitated towards me, everyone wanting to observe this tiny, cute thing who knew how to ham it up. Adults stood up from their seats and walked towards the spectacle of my creation.

It strikes me that my mom didn't interrupt my instincts, in fact, she instead pulled out her camera and documented the moment. Another photo captures me sitting on my knees, the bottom of my feet sticking out, showing bright white, looking up at a man in faded blue jeans wearing a cowboy hat covering most of his face. The cowboy is handing me a coin. My arm reaches up to take it, but he is also bending down, towards me.

The power of my young body had moved men.

Before you knew it, my mom said, lots of folks were handing me coins. Without hesitation, I took this coin and then the others. There I stood, four years old, dancing barefoot on a boat for money. My mom said I had never been so delighted with myself. The back of the cowboy photo reads, "Sam gets paid for performance 1991 July-Southern Star Boat."

While my dancing performance could be viewed as the genesis of attention seeking from strangers, my history of premeditated flashing commenced at age five when I traveled to my best friend Peter's house on an operation in self exposure. Peter was gorgeous, even in kindergarten, with his dusty blonde hair, Caribbean blue eyes, and crisp collared shirts. Sometimes he wore glasses with oversized circle frames, and he was the fastest boy on the soccer field. I lied to everyone at school, telling my classmates he was my boyfriend, a falsity he never outwardly denied.

Peter and I spent most of our playtime building forts and setting up unsuccessful traps for "wild" animals in our suburban, yet forested backyards. Under piles of damp leaves we hid with mud splotched across our faces as camouflage, waiting to trap wolves that never showed. In the winter we pushed each other down icy banks on plastic saucers until our gloves and boas soaked through, freezing our infant extremities. Eventually, someone's mom would usher us inside to warm up with hot chocolate and an afternoon of *Animaniacs*.

I liked that Peter didn't treat me like a girl, except for when we played house. In his father's office shed underneath the fax machine we kissed on the mouth and snuggled topless. The screeching tones of the machine receiving a document followed by the hum of the printer that forewarned us of adults to come.

I was unaware of the impending impulse the morning of the flashing. Like most days started, I stood holding my mother's shoulders, stepping into a pair of pastel cotton underwear. My arms reached up as she draped a tie-dye cotton dress over my head. The rainbow swirl created a momentary kaleidoscope as it fell over my face. She brushed my hair and added a coordinating headband. After giving me one final look-over, she sent me off to play.

But a few hours later, just as I directed California Roller Baby down the staircase, knowing she would tumble, a thought interrupted my playtime. I heard California Roller Baby's skates creaking back and forth taking her nowhere as she splayed out on the bottom of the staircase as I removed my petite undergarments and stashed them behind my dresser.

*Peter has to see this*, I thought holding up my dress and looking down at myself. *Peter needs to see this* my brain shouted as I thudded down the carpeted stairs feeling a rug burn start on my thighs and butt.

"I'm going to Peter's to play," I said to my mom while I propped California Roller Baby up on the kitchen table, adjusted her sunglasses and patted down her hair like a good mother.

"Be home for lunch, don't make me have to call over," my mom said, fixing my headband once more and kissing my cheek.

The front door to Peter's house was open.

"Hello," I said into an empty hallway.

"Hey honey," Mrs. Brown shouted from the living room. I waved and watched as she folded piles of laundry sorted by color. Ricky Lake's voice squawked through the living room. Scents of fresh dryer sheets filled my nose.

"Peter's upstairs," Mrs. Brown said, her eyes fixated ahead at the TV and she shooed me away with a man's grimy white undershirt. As I darted up the staircase and sprinted down the hallway, my limbs stiffened like wooden planks.

"You're out! I shot you three times!" I heard Peter yell. A high-pitched cry erupted from Andrea, his younger sister. Before I could open the door, Andrea kicked it and threw her laser tag vest on the ground. A thud followed as she hurled the heavy plastic gun at the wall.

"It's not fair!" Andrea screamed, stomping one foot. She was three and nothing was ever fair.

"Be nice to your sister!" Mrs. Brown's voice boomed from downstairs. She was an elementary school teacher and had the tone and patience to prove it. Out of breath and running on adrenaline I didn't say hello, try to comfort Andrea, or even take the opportunity to scoop up the laser tag set for myself.

"Look!" I said rolling backwards on the floor as my tie-dye dress flopped over my head. My bare bottom and peach fuzz legs were the only human parts observable.

Underneath the rainbow print I couldn't see their faces, but I heard Andrea sobs dissolve into sniffles.

"Look at this!" I said again. A few more seconds of silence passed before I toppled over, my body aching from the contorted position. I flopped out into a criss cross-apple sauce position.

"You're not allowed to do that!" Peter screamed. His shouting caught me off guard. This was the same boy with whom I took turns putting our butts directly on his dad's copy machine. An unfamiliar ache hollowed my heart. I chewed on the inside of my cheek. At five, my mouth didn't know *betrayal*.

"She's not wearing any underwear!" Peter screamed down to his mother. He belted out *underwear* like the last word of a song. Quick footsteps turned into a patter on the creaking staircase and when I looked up Mrs. Brown was staring down at me. Within seconds she ordered me home to "finish getting dressed." Unfazed by the embarrassment of those around me, I left wondering about the hysteria.

I wasn't sure why they didn't like to look. But I took a mental note on the production I conjured, impressed with the circus and intensity of emotions.

\*\*\*

The psychological history of flashing, or as it's more often written about, *exhibitionism*, is rooted in the drive for sexual pleasure, mainly from a person, usually male, showing their genitals to a stranger. In a diagnostic framework, exhibitionism is often accompanied by masturbation or later masturbation thinking back to the incident. Dysfunction and deviance are common words used in early literature, suggesting a type of mental malfunction on the part of the flasher. Arousal is listed as a typical side effect of the behavior. My original exhibitionist acts didn't bring about any sexual tingles in my body. The sex of it all from the early diagnosis reeks of early American Puritan beliefs, which is both unsurprising and uninspiring. A pattern exists in early American psychology where namely white-Anglo men categorized any behavior with nudity or taboo (homosexuality, cross-dressing, fetishes, for example) as a form of sexual deviance.

While most literature points to flashing as an act seen predominantly among males, female recording of the behavior derives back as early as the 12th and 13th centuries when several Latin historians first recorded variations of Godiva's ride.[1] While highly contested, a historical legend claims Lady Godiva, as an act of protest to her husband's high taxation on the common people, took pity on her subjects and rode horseback naked through the streets of Coventry. The act garnered attention to the cause and allowed the people of Coventry to view Lady Godiva as more ethical and unaligned with her husband. Her act of flashing was an expression of rebellion and unity, unrelated to her sexual drive. In the late 20th century, the phrase *Lady Godiva syndrome* was coined in the later 20th century to describe women who engaged in flashing. The perversion of Lady Godiva's political act is jarring, and shows early on, the historical misinterpretation of women's self-exposure.

Being neither a political activist nor sexual deviant,

early academic writings on exhibitionism feel irrelevant to any of my own experiences. If anything, slinking off my tank top straps and feeling fresh air on my skin made my body electric. A buzz of aliveness diffused through my limbs.

As a girl I fell in love with my body's ability to cause chaos.

\*\*\*

I heard the final whistle screech while underwater. It made me kick faster, knowing practice was over for the morning. Standing soaked and chilled, I huddled with the other kids watching through chlorine logged eyes as Ariel, our coach, ended practice with a pep talk for our upcoming meet. Her hammer toe grazed my foot as she paced the pool deck.

"Be at Briar Ridge 90 minutes early," she said waving us away, breaking the huddle, her long blonde hair flowing in the morning breeze showing a tint of green, which could only have been accumulated by decades steeped in chlorine. "We have the first practice slot. Please no last season suits." Groans erupted; at the beginning of the season everyone preferred their old worn - in racing suits, broken in already from a season's worth of water, they felt like our second skin. "And please, don't eat a bunch of crap before the meet. You have plenty of time for that after your races. Practice dismissed!" We ran, the sound of feet beating over the cement pool decks reverberating, towards the late morning.

After practice, a mess of us would race around the playground in our damp suits and bare feet telling secrets tucked inside plastic tunnels and devouring sour straws before 10 AM I licked the thick coat of sugar off my fingers like a cat, never being sure I hadn't swallowed a few bits of sand. In the early morning of those summer days, I stood fully present in my near naked body. Joy was easy to find in my flat chested, pre-period frame. My body was compliant and felt safe out in the world. I took it all in; a shiver from the icy water or burning feet on scalding pavement as I made my way to my mom's car. I was present with a mind focused on the task at hand; running, yelling, eating, laughing, splashing, and being.

By twelve, I knew what my body could do, and I wanted to see its impact on those around me, especially since it was no longer housed in a preschool body, so I started flashing neighbors.

It was easier than you'd think. My parents, in the final stages of preparing for our trip to the Grand Canyon, wanted me and my five-year-old brother in peak hiking condition. Some nights after dinner, we walked the neighborhood in our new hiking books, carrying backpacks. My best friend from across the street, Catie, accompanied me on these walks where we lagged ten feet behind everyone and gossiped about middle school drama.

One evening towards the end of summer my family plus Catie headed out on a post dinner stroll. I sucked fresh summer corn out of my teeth while Catie sucked on a firecracker popsicle. By this time in our training, my boots were well worn, not a blister remained. My back had grown accustomed to the weight of the Camelback backpack. I slurped and spit out the water, liking how it sounded crashing against the pavement.

"You should steal one of your mom's cigarettes. We can smoke it this weekend during our sleepover," I whispered to Catie. I never inhaled the Virginia Slim, but I liked flicking the lighter on and pulling in the initial drag.

"We'll see. Sometimes she counts them," Catie said. Her mom, hardly five feet tall, was a mean Irish woman with window rattling screams. After work she sat on the side corner of their garage in a folding chair, chain-smoking and fussing at neighborhood kids who biked too fast or talked too loudly. On occasion, she'd flick off minivans for similar trespasses, always acting as the red - headed troll to pass on your way down the block. Despite an intimate knowledge of the rage that rained down on Catie, I spent our childhood putting her in unsavory situations.

The sun continued to hang high even though it had to be past seven when an older man, wearing track pants and oversized headphones power-walked toward my family. His pants swished with every step and a bald spot shined through layers of slicked back gel. Wet air from a thunderstorm earlier in the day coated my throat, tasting like newly poured asphalt. As the man approached, I found myself dropping one strap from my tank top and exposing my left breast. At twelve it was a quarter breast. Not fully formed. This didn't matter as I didn't understand the limitations of my body. An electric thrill shot through me as the damp air hit my freed skin. My guts jolted, similarly reminiscent of what I experienced showing myself to Peter's family.

I attempted eye contact with the power-walking man.

I wanted him to acknowledge my doing and witness his excitement or horror or at least to see him moved. He wouldn't look at me and it appeared he didn't notice, but the act felt powerful. In that moment, I realized the choice of exposing what to whom was mine. Catie shoved me and let out a high-pitched cackle. The sides of her face reddened, matching the tail end of her popsicle.

Creating shock in my mundane world was magic. Soon afterwards, I was dropping down both straps when unsuspecting neighbors neared us during our after-dinner walks. Once an older woman, likely a visiting grandmother, daggered her eyes at me while she huffed past us pushing a baby in a stroller. Another time a teenage boy shouted, "gross!" causing my parents to turn around and check on the commotion. His face squished in disgust as he rolled by on his longboard. The boy's comment and face didn't land. At 11, my world consisted of early aughts Girl Power pop music-Destiny's Child, Christina Aguilera who recently released her most controversial album *Dirty*, and the Spice Girls lingered-a mom who was a loud and proud feminist, not something most mothers were in 2000-and a group of friends who weren't yet boy-crazed. I held my head high, the power of my body feeling stronger than his words.

Twenty-first century research on flashing cites power over another person as an additional function of the behavior.[2] It's noted that men and women both reported feelings of power and dominance over another during the act, but only sometimes did this include arousal. Men compared to women reported higher rates of masturbation attached to flashing.[3] It's now common knowledge that dominance is the primary function of sexual violence towards others, which includes serial flashing and other forms of indecent exposure. No one today thinks Louis C.K. was aroused by office plants or likely even the women he cornered when he masturbated openly without consent. Overwhelmingly, men who feel powerless thrust themselves upon others to regain a semblance of control, while women who feel powerless turn their aggression inwards. Similarly, I learned that just because I was the one removing my top didn't necessarily mean I was the one that felt power. The removal of a garment in and of itself did not always create the sense of dominance.

By the time Aaron stopped by to pick me up for our back to school pool party, it was already dark. It was about to be the start of junior year. My period finally came a few months prior and my body had morphed from shapeless rail to a softness that didn't feel right. Almost overnight I hated how I looked in everything. I'd spent the past hour putting on and taking off every swimsuit I'd owned. Finally, I settled on a tankini, rolled Sofi shorts, and an Abercrombie and Fitch logo tank top.

Porch lights and the occasional passing car acted as the sole artificial light guiding Aaron and my way as we made our way to the pool party. A year prior Aaron started showing up a few afternoons a week to guzzle stolen Natty Lites and listen to my dad's Jimi Hendrix on vinyl. Sometimes we'd smoke weed out of an empty soda can. He wore scratchy ponchos and hemp necklaces. His hair was always greasy, and his breath smelled like Fritos. I liked being around him in the most platonic way. The idea of being pals seemed mutual. He never made a move on me and spent much of our time together talking about his on-and-off again relationship with Molly, another girl in our grade. On our walk to the party, the conversation circled the same old drain of declaring a deep love for her, but never meeting her expectations.

"You can't say you want to hang out with her and then keep canceling to get high with your dumb friends. Of course, she's mad," I said, starting into a familiar riot act.

"Whatever," he huffed, avoiding responsibility and passing me a joint. "Why don't you show me your tits," Aaron said, interrupting my diatribe.

"Gross," I said, shoving him off the sidewalk. He had never flirted with me. The question must have been for shock value.

"No really, come on. Please. Let me just see one," he said, his voice pushy and annoyed.

"One? Who wants to look at one? You're so weird!" I said, squeaking out a laugh, trying to avoid the request while also mentally recounting my past history of singular tit flashing.

"Come on, Sam, I'm sure they're great. I want to see," he said. He stopped walking and I stood three sidewalk blocks in front of him.

He'd never been annoyed with me. He obviously didn't like me like *that*. I felt prudish and immature.

"Fine," I huffed, taking a drag and handing him back the joint.

I held my tank top open from the top and kept my eyes looking out onto the dark road ahead. Seconds later I let go and allowed gravity to drop my shirt back in place.

"Cool, thanks," he said, his voice already changed back to its stoner boy tenor.

Embarrassment twisted throughout my chest and stomach, causing my breath to momentarily shorten. This flashing didn't feel like the other moments that stemmed from an internal need to reveal. I realized Aaron viewed my body as an unattached object available to fulfill his momentary needs. I thought we were friends. Unlike with Peter, I now knew the word for what I felt. At 14, my mouth easily formed *betrayal*. Wanting to escape, I floated out of my skin. No longer did I find my body thrilling to show off. The urge to move out of it overwhelmed me.

Being a female exhibitionist is not the norm. Women are generally not looking for random sexual attention, despite what society continues to state. The mythology surrounding Lady Godiva and her alleged exhibitionism persists today in the continued inability for women to narrate their own stories. Even when a woman tells you exactly what she's doing and why, overbearing patriarchal systems sweep in to diagnose, pathologize, and vilify. From the conservatorship of Britney Spears, the historical cycle of putting women on trial for speaking out (see: Anita Hill, Dr. Christine Blasey Ford, et al.), to the supreme court overturning Roe v. Wade, it's a short stretch to see the continued obsession with controlling and censoring. I never needed documented theories to explain myself.

The idea of power fits better with my perception of flashing. I grew up hungry to create movement in others. Updated risk factors for exhibitionism include a history of sexual abuse and emotional neglect in childhood. I hate to think an act that gave me my first high is an off-shoot symptom of the early childhood sexual abuse I experienced. I want it to be a weird, creative performance of my youth, but the correlation feels logical, a sort of extreme counter behavior to demonstrate the control over my body I had lost.

I think about Diane Arbus at age 15 standing in front of her Upper East Side Manhattan apartment window undressing night after night to the views of strange men from the adjacent building. Diane's childhood consisted of extreme emotional neglect from her parents as well as a confusing sexual relationship with her brother checking off all the exhibitionist prerequisite boxes.[4] Diane wanted to be seen, but it's possible she and others are playing both exhibitionist and voyeur. Maybe she wanted to feel control, but she also wanted to create. As an artist, her photographs captured the evocative, created to provoke reactions. I too wanted to cause momentum. My instinct concedes the act of flashing is more nuanced than the DSM has examined, leaving out the exploration of creative expression.

I kept flashing my body throughout my adolescent and young adulthood. At age 13, I stood barefoot on the outskirts of a soccer field with my best friend Emma, laughing with such velocity that my vision blurred. A neighborhood pool surrounded by a 10-foot-tall metal fence backed up to the soccer field. Inside the fence mothers laid out reading magazines and sipped Diet Cokes while lifeguards whistled at children running too fast. The pool sat on top of a modest but steep hill echoing the sounds of bodies splashing and happy screams out into the neighborhood over half a mile out. Weekend nights the blast of a horn traveled into our home as swim meets took place.

The creaking of adjusting lounge chairs and hiss of sunscreen cans carried into our ears only a few feet away as we let our breasts free. A gust of hot summer wind smacked my stomach and bare chest. The breeze carried a mixture of fresh grass clippings and adolescent perspiration. Emma and I stood with our shirts yanked up to our necks flashing a man operating a riding lawn mower. He ignored us, likely mortified by our underage public display of indecency. Standing shirt up, about to cross the line into full blown puberty, I stood wild and confident in my skin. I didn't know that newfound breasts and hips and changing hormones would usher in an era of discomfort, confusing shame, and a sudden sense of not wanting to be myself. Laughing and shaking my flat chest, I have no idea that I'll spend the next twenty years trying to get back to this moment of being fully present and comfortable in my skin.

# Rumination and Other States I've Known

Ruminating is my brain's preferred state. Early on, I noticed my proclivity towards excessive mulling. I'm more decisive than most and have concluded this is my mind's way of getting back to what it likes best, thinking, manipulating a past moment, turning it over and looking underneath, making sure I haven't missed anything.

As a young girl my mind churned out lists: foods, teachers' first names, book titles, and the song lists from the musical *Annie*. Every night before falling asleep, my brain spit out a list of reasons for which I should be thankful. The list would start, and my mind bulleted the items over and over until I felt like I'd repeated them just so. The listing could take time and pull my attention away from other activities like storytime on the elementary school carpet or center time where I often sat at the writing station jotting down lists and half stories on the back of envelopes. To teachers, I probably appeared day-dreamy.

I didn't always want to be listing, but it made the insides of my temples itchy if I didn't. My mind wouldn't allow me to fantasize about weekend plans like riding bikes or perusing through the mall with friends until I correctly listed. I couldn't say the words too close together, but I also couldn't pause too long in-between. I needed to have the precision of a metronome.

On the bus ignoring my seatmate:

*Blueberry Pop tart, banana, half a peanut butter jelly*
*sandwich, strawberry Nutri-grain bar, fruit cup*
*Blueberry Pop tart, banana*
*Blueberry Pop tart, banana, half a peanut butter jelly*
*sandwich, strawberry*
*Blueberry Pop tart*
*Blueberry Pop tart, banana, half a peanut butter jelly*
*sandwich, strawberry Nutri-grain bar, fruit cup*

****

My mind has long struggled to move on from even the most benign offenses.

On an unseasonably warm autumn day my family and I sat around a wooden picnic table eating cinnamon sugar donuts and drinking apple cider. We'd just finished securing the year's batch of pumpkins, carefully chosen to come home with us to be cut, gutted, and carved. Halloween was big at our house. With dusty powder fingers, I tugged on my dad's arm whining about needing the bathroom.

"Sammy, there are only porta-potties here, do you think you can hold it until we get home?" he said, trying to shield me from my first hole-in-the-ground bathroom experience. I couldn't wait. As we stood in line, my lips pursed, noticing the stench. My dad attempted to give me an informative rundown before he sent me in.

"The poop and pee don't flush. It all stays inside a hole at the bottom. Don't touch the pink bar. It isn't soap. And don't worry about washing your hands," he said prepping me. Our line inched forward. The row of faded blue doors creaked opened and slammed shut with a loud WHAP.

"Okay, your turn. I'll be right here." Inside the humid plastic box, I was promptly traumatized by the receptacle's contents. Without wanting to be inside a second longer than I had to, I didn't even bother wiping myself and opened the door while I finished pulling up my purple velvet leggings. Droplets of warm piss dripped down my thigh.

"Daddy," I yelled, running away from the sight. "Daddy, it's burned in my brain!" I repeated the phrase over and over for fear of knowing this was something I would never shake. He laughed and patted my head as we walked me back to the picnic table.

I can still see that shit today.

Sometimes when I'm ruminating, my mind's voice comes through in a Southern twang, like the way my granny sounded. Born in Tennessee and raised across the Southern half of Virginia, her voice projected her roots. Roots, I believed, were disparate from me. The shame I felt one middle school afternoon when she yelled, "hey punky-diddle" at me from across a Pacific Sunwear in front of shaggy-haired, popular WASPY boys almost knocked me dead on the spot. If I acted up, she hollered: "Samantha Jane, you're working my last nerve!" to let me know the consequences were close. My birth certificate reading *Samantha Denise* never deterred her from calling me *Samantha Jane*. According to my mom, she insisted on using *Jane*, declaring the pairing carried a smoother ring.

One afternoon my granny drove my friend and me to our afternoon dance class. As we buckled in, she turned around and asked, "Sammy, where'd you get those spiffy britches?" The word *spiffy* and *britches* rolling out of her mouth with a heavy drawl jabbed my eardrum and twitched my left eye.

"No one says britches, granny," I hissed back wanting to tuck and roll out of the car. "They're jeans and I got them at American Eagle," I said, rolling my eyes and hoping my friend wouldn't count this embarrassing comment against me.

After these Southern exposures, I made a point to quit saying *y'all* and tried to mind my lazy vowels in order to sound neutral, not wanting to belong to any particular origin. Despite my efforts, I still slur a bit, especially if excited. If I'm not careful I'll let out a "why" instead of "while" or commit the biggest Jewish sin of singing out a "A-men" instead of "Ah-men." Over time, I changed my voice on the outside, molding it to fit better into what I thought I was supposed to be, but on the inside my brain ran ragged in a twanged tenor.

My ruminating thoughts remember the first time I experienced the bliss of terror blended into delight. I spent the night at my cousin Daisy's house. She was three years older than me, and I referred to her family as my *country cousins*. They felt different than me, with their Southern accents, Jesus knick-knacks, and fresh deer meat packed into their freezer. My uncle, a man with a thick beard whose uniform of khaki pants and a button up Columbia shirt was foreign to my concept of *dad*, was my mom's oldest brother. My uncle and his family lived deep in the woods, surrounded by outdoor dogs and a sky darker than I knew existed. No streetlights, passing cars, or neighbor's kitchen lights could be seen from their front porch. Their property at night was black and silent, like the beginning of the horror movies I secretly watched at home Saturday nights. My uncle, an avid naturist and hunter, spent the weekend touting my cousin and me around their land to observe his process post-hunt.

Understanding the cycles of nature was a value he worked to instill in us. He took my cousin and me to see the freshly shot deer in his shed. I watched as he strung up his most recent kill with the gentleness of tying a child's shoelaces. He lassoed the animal's slender ankles and hung the deer up leaving the animal's front hooves almost scraping the ground.

"I'll use all of this animal, snout to tail," he said, tracing the animal's skin with a hunting knife. While I didn't understand what he meant, I knew he didn't take death lightly. Standing a few feet away bundled in a cardinal red puffer coat with my hands crammed into scratchy mittens, I didn't notice the cold of the winter night. I stood, transfixed watching the blood, thicker than any syrup I'd ever poured, drain from the animal forming a gluey pool below. My hands tingled from the arousal of seeing shiny innards and glistening organs. I've been chewing on the sight of those guts ever since.

This twangy rumination has access to the feeling of cold water cutting across my stomach as I waded through a creek spreading mosquitoes with my hand like a knife to hot butter. It feels twigs crunching underneath my sneaker soles and the sting of a grass blade as I try to whistle it between my thumbs. It knows how coarse sand feels being brushed off the back of my knees and the burn of warm salt rushing through my nose and lungs as I'm working underneath an ocean wave. My body's twang has memorized the texture of sticky aloe lotion lathered on burnt shoulders and frozen popsicles inside my desperate summer mouth.

This twang also recalls hands on my body, unwanted hands coming at me without consent. It relieves the smoothness of them; young hands with too long nails, dirt crusted. I might spend the rest of my life thinking about those boys' hands.

Around age seven my ruminating mind transformed from distraction to physical pain. At night I'd close my eyes searching for sleep, but my mind would begin ticking, thinking, and listing. One night the thinking ran too fast and too far from me, sucking all the air from my lungs. I asphyxiated in my thoughts. In the moment, my pea-sized brain believed the thinking would kill me.

I forced my body to sit up and directed my legs to walk down my bunk bed ladder

step          by        step.

Then directed them to journey another

step          by        step

down our wooden staircase. I stood staring at my parents through the banister hoping they would know what was wrong.

"What's up, bug? Do you feel sick?" my mom asked looking up from the couch. It was unusual for me to be out of bed. I was not a child who asked for endless glasses of water or made up excuses to not go to bed. She stood and walked to the bottom of the staircase waving me to come all the way down.

"I don't want to be a human bean," I said, my voice cracking, but not crying.

My mom looked over at my dad who shrugged and let out an uneasy laugh. My mom pulled me towards her body, pressing my skull into her chest and stroking my hair.

"I don't want to die," I said.

"Honey, your dad and I are not going to die for a very, very long time, and you aren't going to die for an even longer time. You don't have to worry," she said, full of parental assurance.

She kissed me and I climbed back up the staircase

step           by        step.

Then up my bunk bed ladder

step           by        step.

I tucked myself back into bed, none the less panicked.

Racing thoughts and anxiety before bed along with difficulty falling asleep are both hallmark indicators of Post-Traumatic Stress Disorder. Of course, my parents couldn't have known I was experiencing these symptoms; they didn't know I had experienced any trauma to have developed PTSD.

Back in bed I reached for a new remedy: prayer. It was an act my mom used to perform over me before tucking me in for the night, but we hadn't done it together in years. She would stand beside my beds with folded hands and her chin down toward her chest. I couldn't remember any of the words she said, but in my limited memories she appeared calm and relaxed. Those prayers were the last time I could remember an easy night's sleep, so maybe that was what I was missing.

Laying on my back like a mummy I clasped my hands and closed my eyes. I thanked god for my family, friends, teachers, neighbors, and all the good things I had in my life. I told god I loved him so much. Then with an air kiss I blew my words upwards and hoped they would reach him. Afterwards I felt calmer and went to sleep without feeling strangled by my mind.

The next night, I was ready. I clasped my hands again, closed my eyes, and let the words tumble out of my mouth. Unlike the night before, my nerves didn't feel better after I finished. Maybe I didn't say it right, so I tried again. Maybe I said it too fast, so I said it again making sure to enunciate every name. By the end of the week the prayer was taking 20 minutes to get through. For the next eight years I tried getting the prayer to work its magic, chasing the dragon, but never again did it unburden me the way it did the first night.

*Dear god,*

*Thank you so, so, so much for today. I am so thankful for my mom, dad, brother, my grandma, grandpa, and granny, my aunts, uncles, cousins, Miss Margaret, her son Jayden, his older sister Stacey. Thank you for Ms. Shannon and her kids Tyler, Nick, and Janet. I am thankful for my family and friends. I love you so, so, so much. Amen*

Nick, my babysitter's son, was the boy sexually assaulting me, even though I didn't have a concept or language for it at the time. I did know he had been touching me, and I didn't like it. I did know I'd said, "no," and it kept happening anyway. Despite all this, knowing, I thanked god for him every night.

# 40 oz. Till Freedom

I craned my neck down the hallway acting as lookout while Emma lifted a bottle of vodka from her brother's underwear drawer. It was around 8pm during a sleepover mid-summer. We were five weeks out from the start of high school and while most of our friends already secured a handful of drinking parties neither one of us had swallowed more than a few sips of a wine cooler. I knew the two of us gagging down room temperature vodka wouldn't be the social event of the year, but I felt hopped up on the excitement of doing anything that brought me one step closer to my imagined adult life.

Emma lived adjacent to my solidly middle-class neighborhood. Her neighborhood was good old Southern money; the kind of Southern homes with monogrammed towels, BMW and Range Rover lined driveways, blue-blooded families, and streets lined with 90's McMansions. Emma's house was no exception. Her manicured lawn and perfectly trimmed hedges were kept up by her mother, who could be found pruning in a full face of make-up with gold hoops hanging from her ears and a thick gold chain dripping around her neck, all while in a thick cable knit sweater and pressed slacks. The interior of the home was sprawling with a fully finished basement and a formal living room adorned with white antique furniture that we weren't allowed to breathe on. The best feature was Emma's bedroom, which resided on a different floor from her parents. In the unnecessary privacy of what felt like an entire wing, we spent our adolescent years roaming chat rooms for cyber-sex, taking racy photos, downloading dick pics, and starting drama amongst our friends via AIM.

We waited to break into the vodka until we were sure everyone was asleep. Holding our breath to listen better, we waited for the familiar *click* of the old TV set in the kitchen being turned off by Emma's dad who watched the eleven o'clock news. We strained listening for his feet to shuffle down the hall and finally to hear the bedroom door shut. Sitting criss-crossed on the white carpet of Emma's bedroom floor, we faced each other with the hijacked vodka and a Sprite in between us looking like a deserted game of spin of the bottle. I nodded my head at her and made eyes at the vodka prompting her to take the first swig. I jumped and grabbed Emma's leg at the hiss of the Sprite can. Our nervous laughter filled the room. Emma's face squished in disgust as she passed me the vodka bottle. An unexpected burn coated my lungs, pushing out a cough as I struggled to swallow. My throat fought against me and, for a split second, I was unsure I could force it down. After a few trials, we discovered the tried-and-true method of immediately chasing the vodka with a large gulp of soda. Within minutes my insides warmed, and I felt wholly relaxed in a way I never knew possible. The two of us laughed endlessly; my jaw ached.

The next morning, I awoke with a stiff body and an alerting sense of panic. For a moment I forgot where I was, until I looked over and saw Emma's thick hair sprawled across a pillowcase. I was tucked in Emma's bed wearing a T-shirt I have never seen before. For the first time in my life, I had no recollection of going to sleep. My last memory flashed: the two of us danced around her room blasting the new self-titled Jennifer Lopez album. I recalled twirling and smashing my face into a lamp and seeing Emma sink to the ground howling with laughter. As I touched my face, I felt a momentary sense of relief realizing nothing was bruised or scratched. My hair matted and stunk of vomit. Realizing I was awake, Emma rolled over and asked what I remembered. Her voice was sharp and agitated. I blacked out. According to her, I puked all over her bathroom. I needed to be bathed like a toddler. Emma had spent the entire night checking on me every half hour to check on my breathing. She kept saying how out-of-control I acted. Shame and stomach acid washed through me as I quickly packed up my bag to leave. I couldn't find the words to apologize and left feeling like an idiot for turning a fun night into a burden. All day I threw up bile hunched over in pain. My stomach felt like it had been scraped with a Brillo pad. I didn't understand how she escaped the evening unscathed.

*** 

Austin played the bass, donned heavy metal T-shirts, had a face full of acne, and wore his stringy, hazel hair a few inches past his shoulders often in a ponytail. Two months into my sophomore year of high school I wrangled him into being my first serious boyfriend. I first noticed him because he was the new kid. The new kids were easy to spot in a building full of faces that I had seen since at least middle school and some since elementary. Then I noticed the way he sat in the back of class doodling and reading books, not attending the lectures but adding the occasional comment to show everyone he was smart. He had a vile sense of humor; at least once a week I keeled over in laughter from one of his offhanded comments. One afternoon he attempted to have an open discussion with our teacher regarding felching, leaving her with a beet red face and the rest of us roaring. During class I passed Austin notes which vacillated between fawning (*you're the cutest new guy our school has had in years*) and ego stomping (*everyone thinks your T-shirts make you look like a poser. You should probably cut your hair. Is it true you failed out of your old school?*) When he showed interest, I would push him away and rotate to acting pouty when he didn't pay attention to me. I had been perfecting this hot-cold method since elementary school and continued to use it throughout college. When used with the correct ratio of Madonna to whore, this technique has a success rate of 85%.

After school Austin journeyed on his busted dirt bike the three miles to my house so we could be alone before my parents came home from work. A routine evolved; we would make small talk for five minutes, I'd offer him a snack, which he always declined, and then we'd go upstairs to my room to make out until I heard my dad's minivan turning right onto our street. We both had to put our hair back into ponytails when we kissed. He never needed to borrow a hair tie. The minutes of kissing stretched out like hot taffy. Kissing with tongues and touching bodies was new for me. Before Austin I had only kissed one other boy with tongue, and it lasted less than 30 seconds and we had stood at least a foot apart. I liked this kissing; it felt easy, and for the first time I felt turned on by someone other than my imagination. I liked being wanted.

These easy make out sessions went out for what seemed like endless afternoons, until they didn't. On one routine afternoon, just kissing was no longer enough. I don't remember what band T-shirt Austin wore or what lie I told my mom about my ongoing activities for the afternoon. We must have just started kissing because our bodies were still upright, sitting on the edge of my bed. An immediate sense of apprehension sparked my brain, putting me on high alert as his hand left my back and snaked around to the front of my shirt. His hands hadn't ever left my back, other than to sometimes put his hand on my ass, but in general it never felt like they were heading to a new location. Pausing, he hovered an open palm on top of my stomach. I felt my breaths shallowing out against his hand. He proceeded to move his fingers upward in a steady, methodical manner, then slipping his hand under my shirt and running his fingers over my skin. His hand reached the back of my bra. As if his fingers pads were bolts of lightning, I shot up and jumped back. My brain felt dizzy, and my mind spun. It felt like I was drowning as I made my way to the floor, leaning my back against my bed and letting my head drop between my knees while I hyperventilated.

Austin rubbed my shoulders and told me I was okay. When he spoke, his voice reverberated into my eardrums like I was submerged underwater. *It's probably just nerves*, he said reassuring me, *since you've never really done anything with a guy before*. Nerves were what happened before a big test or what I felt when the music started at a dance competition.

I was suffocating, but I nodded as he talked and steadied myself.

Austin offered to stay, saying we could take a walk or listen to music, but I wanted him gone. I was embarrassed and confused about what felt like a betrayal by my body. After he left, I tried to focus on homework, but my mind flashed clips of a boy from my early childhood. His hands coming towards me. The relaxed verbal reminder to shut the door. Walking up the ladder on his bunk bed. Over and over and over and over I walked up that ladder feeling the cool, smooth wood on my palms and petite bare feet. Another flash: His older sister opening the door to tell us it was time for lunch and pausing, noticing something was not quite right. *Help me* my insides screamed. *Tell me I can't be in here alone anymore.* I never yelled. I was always church mouse quiet. I shut my eyes trying to dissolve the images. My skin tightened, and my stomach turned as I stared into a textbook not reading a word. For years, I fantasized about having a zipper at the back of my neck for when these feelings crept up. It would be a much easier out.

The next afternoon Austin arrived bearing gifts. *Look what I got* he said holding up four sweaty Budweisers hanging from a six-pack container. *Where are the other two?* I asked, pretending to be annoyed. *This was the only thing left in my dad's fridge* he said jumping onto the front porch stirring with the pride of a man who had just come back from a successful hunt. *It should help you relax*, he said. We drank the lukewarm cans in my room while he forced me to listen to a band I didn't care about. My eyes watched the colors of the CD mix as it revolved through the top of the boombox, reminding me of a spin art toy I cherished as a child. Halfway through the first beer my body felt heavy, calmer. After the second I became silly and cozy in my skin. I wanted to be touched. We made out carelessly all afternoon exploring each other's skin all without feeling like I needed to run. I guided his hand up my shirt showing him I was okay.

With booze I figured out a way to be comfortable within my body and be the girlfriend I was supposed to be. When Austin left, I hid the cans in my neighborhood's trash cans and then started my homework. I completed the assignments, still buzzed, and while it wasn't my best work, my mind was empty. No flashes from the past jolted through my skull. I could breathe. All of the thoughts inside of me were dull and numb which, for the first time, I realized was maybe all I ever wanted. Alcohol. It was so simple.

I finished my work, feeling like I'd solved the problem of myself.

# The Looking Glass Complex

Moms are like babies; everyone thinks theirs is the most beautiful. But my mom was stunning, objectively. In her thirties she won a Princess Diana look-alike contest; she exuded that kind of obvious beauty. She was slim but strong and toned. Her cheekbones popped and her face seemed to glow.

As a kid I loved watching her apply lipstick on her way out to work. Pausing in the mirror, like the act was an afterthought, she would draw a coral circle around her lips in one swoop and make an audible pop with her mouth. I liked hearing the clacking of her heels as she hurried down our wooden staircase in the morning. Even in her tired sweatshirts and baggy jeans she emanated cool. She felt important to be around.

To watch as she verbally assaulted herself felt sacrilegious. I couldn't wrap my brain around her point of view. Her inability to appreciate herself made it impossible for me to decipher what was true regarding self-worth. Her failure to distinguish reality incited a resentment towards her. It made her words ungraspable and weightless. It left me examining the world as a funhouse mirror. By the time I was in college, her opinions carried no weight and I mocked any of her attempts at advising me.  If I felt any way for her, it was a pity for her low self-esteem. In the narcissism of my youth, I couldn't see we were emotional mirror images.

***

I mentally recited my speech when I arrived home from work. The second my foot touched our hardwood, I reached behind me, unhooking my bra and tossing it on the back staircase. Wearing outside clothes inside has always been impossible for me. I threw my shoes in the same spot while working up the nerve to tell my mom I needed to ask her something. The back staircase was a catch-all in our home for items removed in a hurry: shoes, socks, bras, backpack, pocketbooks.

"This isn't a closet," my mom would yell from the bottom of the stairs while chucking a pair of sneakers at me as I passed in the hallway above. I decided the conversation could wait until dinner. Between a forkful of something less than 13 Weight Watchers points and discussions about upcoming summer schedules, I dropped the question as a statement.

"I think I want to stay home instead of going to the beach next month. None of the other new counselors take more than one day of vacation during the summer and I want them to hire me again for next summer." In reality, my intent to stay home revolved around a commitment to drinking and bringing boys back to the house at the end of a long day. I looked at my mom, trying to speculate her thoughts by observing how she held her face. She looked down at her plate. I looked at my dad who looked at my mom. Then, in a surprising non-moment, my mom said I could stay: "You're 19 and have just spent a year on your own. I think you can manage a week."

Three weeks later I watched my parents pack up the car. Boogie boards and plastic beach toys displayed through the rear window. Parker, my younger brother, was disappointed I wasn't coming, and I felt a twinge of melancholy staring into his round, pale, freckled face. It hit me as I looked into his bright blue eyes and tousled his dark hair: I had never missed a family vacation and I knew there would be fewer opportunities as the years wore on.

My melancholy dissipated as I watched the van leave the driveway. In the quiet of my family home, I felt giddy, like when Macaulay Culkin first realizes he has the house to himself. A few hours later, alone at the dinner table I sent up a faux prayer thanking god for "the lovely cheese pizza just for me" and cracked open a bottle of wine, also just for me. Over the next four days I lived in the conflicting states of intoxication or hangover. But I felt content, and it was nice to relax into my momentary truth without hiding.

Near the end of the week, I had a few people over from school. With eight people I considered it a gathering. Nothing about our beer pong or tame card playing could have qualified the evening as a party, especially compared to the ragers we'd grown accustomed to back at school in damp basements filled with wall-to-wall bodies. One of my friends brought over a guy named Brett, whom I was not friends with but had seen around. He didn't ask if Brett was welcome, but I decided he could stay, even though my stomach punched around trying to tell me to send him home. I ignored my stomach's hunch even though I knew Brett was a loose cannon. Brett was wasted when he arrived, but I'd never seen him sober, so his demeanor itself wasn't jarring. His drinking looked different. Even amongst us 20-year-old binge drinking coeds, he looked like an alcoholic. Booze disappeared around him; I can't recall him taking a sip of anything. Within less than an hour, Brett became difficult to contain inside the house, despite my pleas about the late hour and quiet streets. He was determined to stay on the back porch, even after I promised him that he could smoke inside.

Two police cars silently pulled up and parked on my front lawn. Red and blue strobe through the kitchen and entryway. One of my neighbors called the police, citing excessive noise and suspicion of underage drinking. *This will be the end of my summer*, I thought flashing forward to my parents learning about the events that were about to unfold. The officers knocked loudly, just like in the movies. They took us all to my back porch and lined us up, breathalyzing us one by one. The moments before the knock we all sucked on pennies, at the frantic promise from someone it would lower our BAC. Waiting to blow, the coins rolling around my mouth tasted like blood. The officer handed me my own phone and forced me to call my parents. As a young middle-class white woman, I was more terrified of my parents evoking their power to constrict my social life more than I was of the police. Subconsciously, I knew this incident wouldn't destroy my future. Correctly, I assumed it would merely involve community service and court fees.

My parents left Myrtle Beach as soon as my mom got off the phone with the cops. They had the whole 8-hour drive back to think about what a destructive, irresponsible daughter they raised. In the meantime, my mom called her best friend Linda and husband Mitch, who was a longstanding cop, to pick me up and take me to their home for the night. Having a babysitter was no longer optional. I spent the night in their guest room wide awake, sobbing and replaying the events of the past year and realizing there was more to explain than the current underage drinking ticket.

"Obviously you can't manage a week alone," my mom said during the late night phone call. Her anger and lack of surprise regarding my behavior and choices exploded any remaining sense of self I retained. Our relationship was far away from me fawning over her daily routines and fixed admiration. I couldn't pinpoint the moment it grew complicated. My life at this point was holding together about as well as a book with no binding. Since the start of spring semester, I began breaking compact mirrors into shards to employ against myself; a habit I promised myself I'd quit after high school graduation. More nights than not, I spent hovering around a keg until my mind emptied of thoughts. For lent, I vowed to my best friend to give up hooking up with guys, cold turkey.

"I need to take 40 days off from any sexual physical contact. Even kissing. I need you to supervise me when we're out. If you even see me looking at a guy twice, please yell at me."

A week later she quit her role as supervisor when she opened the door to me, yet again, shirtless and kissing a lacrosse player. "It's just light kissing, I swear!" I yelled from the lap of a guy whose name I did not know. "I should really go," I said politely, removing myself from him, redressing, and heading for the door.

"If it's making you feel gross, I don't understand why you're doing it," my friend asked, annoyed, as we lined up shots on the sticky kitchen counter.

"Me either," I said, sucking back piss-colored tequila.

While I hoped this summer would be a break from it all, I was finding it hard to control my anxiety and hid my drinking from my parents. I couldn't keep everything a secret anymore and decided since my parents were already going to be mad at me, I might as well throw on another hefty scoop of disappointment by telling them how much I was struggling.

***

On the front porch of our house, I sat on our white wicker rocking chair pumping myself back and forth while my mom paced round and round in front of me. Her bare feet pounded across the porch and an occasional *creak* escaped from a spot of warped wood. The sky blazed orange as the sun set and the cicadas buzzing rattled my eardrums. Summer was closing in on us. Never had I seen my mom's eyes so narrow or her stare so precise. I wasn't sure if she was going to hug me or hurl me off the porch. My chin rested on top of my knees, which were pulled up to my chest. I felt small and childlike rocking in the chair.

"I need to tell you something," I said before my mom could choose. Without a practiced speech my mouth opened and the words spilled out of me like hot soup: the drinking, cutting, the secret therapist, and somehow, I even managed to describe what happened to me at the babysitter's house as a child and how everything I was dealing with now felt connected to being back in that house. I watched my words scalding my mom as her eyes welled and silent tears began to fall down her cheeks. She reached out for me. Buried in her chest I felt her body shaking in surged heaves.

My shoulders dropped half a foot; I didn't know I needed to be held.

Stepping away from me, my mom turned and walked back inside. I relaxed my body into the rocking chair, chipping away at the paint on the wicker to reveal the natural brown. Paint chips gathered around my nails, I didn't want to ruin it, but I couldn't stop. Both of my parents appeared at the front door.

"Tell your dad what you just told me," my mom said with wet eyes and a crumpled face. I spoke in short vague sentences while I watched my mom continue to cry. My dad said he was sorry and gave me a hug. Then he looked at my mom and waited. He shifted his weight and nudged her. Familiar cars drove by our home. The *whoosh* of skateboard wheels echoed nearby.

"You can call my school therapist," I said, noticing the shift in mood. I had started seeing a therapist in the second semester when my best friend threatened to call my mom and tell her I was cutting again.

"I never wanted to have to tell you this," my mom started.

"Your mom has talked to and helped a lot of other women," my dad added.

"I know how you're feeling," she said. "When I was young, the same thing happened to me. It went on for a long time. And more than anything, I never wanted this to happen to you." She explained the who and the what of it all, and I watched my dad nod and put his hand on her shoulder for support.

Later that night as I brushed my teeth, I couldn't hold eye contact with myself in the mirror. A complex was born, making it painful for me to view myself. I was thinking about my parents knowing. The feeling of relief from not carrying around this secret was short-lived and replaced by a sense of being too seen. I worried that the knowing would cause others to see the disgust that I felt. I worried if people knew what happened they would picture it happening to me and would associate me with the images. I didn't want anyone to see what I couldn't tolerate myself.

At 19 I didn't know Virginia Woolf self-diagnosed herself with a "looking glass complex," which she understood as an inability to look at herself in the mirror. Woolf scholar DeSalvo theorized that when Woolf looked at herself in a mirror,[1] she saw the grotesque sexual abuse she had endured. I wish I'd known about this theory as a way to feel less alone. It would have been nice to know this anxiety was a common symptom. While I felt overly exposed, I did begin to understand, for the first time while trying to look at myself, why my mom couldn't always take photos with us or accept compliments or say nice things about herself. In a moment where I felt distance from her, our throughlines of abuse and self-hate felt like a connection.

The abuse, the explicitness, was difficult to look at. As I tried again to hold my own gaze my mind spun, and it felt like I was finally able to piece together a puzzle that I had attempted to organize my whole life while blindfolded. Actions, words, and memories all at once began clicking into tidy places where before they bounced around with anger, not fitting into any previous idea I had about my mom. The need to control us out of a sense of safety. Her suspicion about the world being a scary place. Her openness about sex and sexuality. The books about good touch and bad touch. Her anxiety. Her relationship with food. Her self-loathing. All of it clicked and for the first time I understood her. Maybe, I thought, I could start understanding myself too.

# Lay Bare

The summer of 2008 was an emotional marathon. Not only did I get ticketed by the police for underage drinking, tell my parents about the sexual abuse I experienced as a child, and work 40 hours a week while hungover, but I also felt the dormant impulse to undress. Fantasies about strip clubs itched my mind.

In my mind, strippers exuded confidence and power, both of which I wanted. It unnerved me realizing my body insecurity was not a phase I could shake off. This young woman who pulled at her stomach and cried over half a pound on the scale was not who I was supposed to be. I had spent my life fantasizing about living my adult life as a successful, lively, independent woman like Kate Hudson in every early 2000's rom-com.

Spring semester of my sophomore year I began what I collegiately dubbed *social experiments* where I'd tuck my dress into my underwear and time how long it took for someone to tell me.

Sometimes I'd let a nipple pop out of a tank top midconversation to see who reacted and how. Unlike my childhood flashing days, these moments didn't provide a sharp increase in dopamine, aside from the few laughs garnered, likely because I was self-anesthetized from bottom shelf vodka. Mixed in with the keg stands, beer bongs, and the *Girls Gone Wild* debauchery, my slight acts of exhibitionism blended into the background of collegiate Greek Life.

I'd hoped twenty would be the marker of a new era

where I'd transform into a bonafide, takes no shit from no one, confident woman. Despite this pipe dream, the clock striking midnight and ushering in the dawn of a new decade didn't alchemize me into a new woman. After a night out of typical 21st birthday shenanigans - rounds of lemon drops, a sash declaring Finally 21, and light hazing from friends - I continued to feel like a drunk, depressed child whose only skill was maintaining a 3.9 GPA. It seemed impossible that I had lived in this state of self-loathing for the past seven years. In high school as I watched self-worth fade away, I'd assumed it would boomerang back, and that this bout of insecurity was a part of typical girlhood development.

"You're allowed to make more money than your husband," my mom said to me one night as she sipped a glass of white wine and stirred mixed vegetables over a steamy stove wearing a wrap dress with a full face of makeup, unmoved from the day. While she wasn't our home's technical breadwinner, she routinely maintained anywhere between 1-2 money making side gigs, outside of her full time job as an optometrist, ensuring that we could afford extras that she didn't have as a child: plane travel, any extracurricular activity we wanted, summer camps, popular name brand clothing, and dinners at restaurants and ordering in whenever the mood struck. I never doubted that Mom could have taken care of herself if needed. "You should always have enough money to leave," she said another evening during a car ride to our yoga class while singing along to Madonna's *Ray of Light*. While I'd huff and roll my eyes at these declarations, the reflex of adolescent girls, I filed her words away in my brain never too far from reach. By my late teens my mind cemented the notion that I would grow up to be financially independent and capable.

But as I slouched through my early twenties, staring at the edge of impending adulthood and the end of the safe structure of the formal education system, I realized I needed to take drastic action to be the woman I had longed envisioned instead of the self-conscious, anxious person who worried over everyone else's thoughts of me.

The idea of stripping was never correlated to the pleasure of men. Imagining the stiff bodies and hairy limbs attached to men left me unenticed, but I craved a sense of power and control with them. My dad's sister, 18 years my senior, worked as a Hollywood make-up artist and acted as a close confidant throughout my childhood. We spoke almost every day from ages 14-20 via AIM. During my summer weeks spent in Los Angeles visiting my grandparents, she would rescue me from their vanilla neighborhood of Thousand Oaks, scooping me up in her yellow VW Beetle to whisk me away to the counterculture of West Hollywood. Over bowls of hot Pho, she would launch into pro-sex diatribes, musing to me about the importance of kink, sex worker dignity, and the need to decriminalize pot. On a car ride through Laurel Canyon, she played me Johnny Cash's "Hurt," knowing what I'd done to my skin, assuring me I wasn't alone. Listening to the lyrics, I shrank into the front seat of her VW beetle and stared out of the window pretending I was engrossed in the houses on the hill. Art, she preached, could be found in the same pain that drove destruction. As we drove, she talked about how she acquired a STD during her twenties and how it was important to talk about the hard topics, even the ugly topics, to destigmatize them. According to my aunt, sex was an act between people (or persons) occurring for a spectrum of reasons, mostly pleasure, but none having to be love. I filed away this information, placing it next to the idea from my mother, who proclaimed true love made sex meaningful, and began forming my own thoughts on what being a woman could be.

With this amalgamated education, I imagined strip clubs as places to conjure sexual power and be on display. I wanted to give men what they wanted, and I fantasized about doing it without the charade, without the heels, hair twirls, or G-strings. I imagined removing my plain clothes with an unmade face. Look at me, shout degrading expletives at me, whistle, tell me you want me to fuck you, and give me all the cash in your wallet.

Maybe, I thought, a strip club could save me. The club could give me confidence and an ability to reclaim my skin. Knowing I would be wanted would have to help the way in which I viewed my body. I needed validation and I figured if I couldn't get it from the inside, the outside was a good enough place to start.

As soon as my family left for Myrtle Beach, days before the police would call and bring them back, they left me home alone under the assumption that I'd continue working as a camp counselor and look after the house. On their first night away, I pleaded with Scott, my on-again-off-again boyfriend, to pick me up and drive me downtown for an impromptu interview at our local strip club, Paper Moon. As a small girl I stared at the building, tracking it with my eyes from the backseat of my dad's four door Chrysler as long as I could, feeling a building sense of excitement. My heart raced wondering what occurred inside the beige rectangle trimmed in dark purple. The lack of windows only added to the intrigue. The purple signage in front of the building showed the words "Paper Moon" in neon pink writing with an outline of a thin, busty woman sitting inside a crescent moon. As the building vanished from my sight, I felt the familiar sense of frustration regarding the mysteries surrounding the adult world.

Although I could have driven myself, I insisted Scott accompany me. Perhaps subconsciously I longed for him to know I never believed my body had been solely for his eyes and hands. Scott was my first of many romantic milestones and although I was never in love with him, I liked keeping him within arm's reach.

At 18, a year prior, I had heaved my virginity at Scott, wanting to get rid of it like it was a hex needing to be expelled. Scott and I spent the summer before I went away to college swapping "I love you's," orgasms, and drugs. Most Sunday afternoons Scott and I would get high on whatever one of us could scrounge up, pills, weed, or beers and watch movies in his parent's dank basement. Hours later we'd emerge to sit down for Sunday supper with his folks trying to act sober but giving ourselves away by laughing too loud or holding court with tangent stoner babble. Our relationship felt like a pair of well-worn jeans. I worked hard trying to make my "I love you's" true.

Humidity stifled the night as we drove down the main drag of our town towards the strip club. At my request, he removed the doors and windows from his Jeep and passed a skinny joint between us. He let me pick the radio station, and in these easy moments I wished I wanted him.

I wore a cotton, dirt brown sleeveless babydoll dress with stacked sandals. During my late teen years, my wardrobe consisted primarily of preppy clothing flecked with American Eagle and Hollister logos, so this dress, which was probably a beach cover-up, was the most provocative article I owned. The club was a world away, even if the odometer only added five miles, from my suburban neighborhood, in a part of town I knew little about. From the Jeep's open window, I watched as shopping malls became less lit, the Hooters and the old record store popped up, then a car wash, and finally the same day loans storefronts appeared. As a young, white, upper middle-class woman I had the privilege to dip into this seemingly exotic place.

When we pulled into the parking lot, Scott killed the engine but kept his eyes straight ahead as if he was still focused on driving. Low budget storefronts scattered throughout the vast shopping center, half of which were abandoned. The parking lot held fewer than ten cars, and both the sun and moon hung low in the sky. It was too early to be at a strip club.

"Why do you even want to be here? Strippers are practically hookers. The girls inside are a bunch of coke whores. The guys in this part of town don't even have money." As I half listened, I pulled my baking thighs off his seats and worried about the sweat marks on the back of my dress. "You shouldn't be here. You aren't like those girls."

The phrase *those girls* bloomed into a rage inside of my

chest so large I thought my sternum would snap. My mind pieced together an entire thesis on how all women were sex workers. But I knew he couldn't see it, and I kept all of this to myself as I checked my face one last time in the sun visor. As I stood shaking out the remaining sweat marks on my dress, I nodded in false agreement pretending to listen as Scott finished his lecture before heading inside.

Inside the club, *those girls* shuffled around in sweatpants, crop tops, and varying degrees of hair and make-up getting organized for the night. The energy of "getting ready" radiated familiarity. Overly fit men in jeans and logoed T-shirts wiped down tables and readied the bar. The crashing of ice being dumped into the ice well momentarily deafened the women's chatter and clinking of glasses. I stared at the stage, which appeared more modest than I imagined. Without the illumination of a spotlight, three gold poles stood equidistant across a black platform, appearing doubled by the mirror lining the wall. I envisioned myself removing articles of clothes, without dancing, without falsifying an ideal of sexy, to a room full of hungry faces. They would cheer whether or not I danced. Right away I wanted to take my clothes off.

A uniformed man approached asking what he could help me with and, in my most professional voice, I explained to him that I had stopped by to drop off my résumé and check if any openings were available for the position of hostess.

"I'm 19," I added, despite him not asking.

"We don't have any jobs. For you," he said, glancing at my résumé and handing it back to me, to which I assumed he meant 19-year-old girls who worked as camp counselors at the local YMCA, lived with her parents, and didn't own a proper pair of heels. Without protest I left. Scott stood outside leaning against his car smoking a cigarette, looking like a guy plucked from any chick flick. His eyes brightened with relief when he noticed me walking towards his car and away from the club. "How was it?"

"They don't want me. No surprise." I said, attempting to hide my disappointment.

"That just means they can tell you're not slutty white trash. It's a good thing." He bounced into the front seat and tossed his cigarette pack into the cup holder. "Strippers are fun, but guys know they're gross. No one wants to marry a stripper." Again, I remained silent letting his ignorant notions fill the car. While I knew he was wrong, I couldn't articulate my thoughts, and it didn't seem like it would be worth the energy even if I could. I often kept my mouth shut for the comfort of others.

"Let's go buy some beers," I said as Scott started the car and handed me a case of CDs to peruse. I landed on Sublime's *Greatest Hits*. "I'm not ready to go home." A short two miles later we had arrived back to the land of manicured lawns, matching minivans, and streetlights. Already I longed for the pink fluorescent lights and aroma of stale beer which I associated with newness and a potential freedom from my old way of being. Scott parked his Jeep in the parking lot of a community pool that strictly prohibited loitering. I guzzled a can and looked out over the pristine soccer field feeling like the losing team.

"My friend Emma and I used to flash the guys who cut

the grass here. We were hardly 13 and we would stand at the top of that hill while the entire pool was full of families right behind us. I don't know if anyone ever noticed."

"I bet the guys trying to cut the grass noticed two girls shaking their tits, " he said, cracking open another can and passing it to me without me having to ask. If it wasn't for those damn *I love yous*.

"We weren't shaking anything. We would just stand there, with our shirts lifted up." I said. I felt it was an important distinction.

"Come here." I said, stepping over the console and settling into the back seat. I needed Scott to want to touch me and to know my body had the power to move men. Without question he climbed into the back seat. For a moment we sat side by side, not touching each other, letting the car fill with the sounds of liquid sloshing in cans and bodies peeling off hot leather.

Kissing Scott tasted familiar, his mouth aromatic of cigarettes and Coke heavy. I ran my palm over his stubbled face as if I was trying to read braille. It never felt right on my fingertips.

Under the safety of our suburban bubble, I realized I would never have a room of men to watch me from afar. I knew I would need a new plan to repair the broken relationship between me and my body, but for the night Scott let me fuck him like a stranger with whom I didn't have a shared history with and, for the moment, it was enough.

# Good and Clean and Fine

I've always felt compelled to rinse myself off at the end of the day. I've never been able to go to bed without cleaning off the filth acquired through a mere 16 hours of living. I'd rather not brush my teeth for 24 hours than not run my body under hot water. This compulsion intensified in the months post attack. At times I was taking two to three showers per day and not coming out until my skin was reddened. The act of washing began to carry a biblical sense of cleansing. Watching my skin turn pink under the steamy water was a way to see a transformation. Every day I imagined I scrubbed off a little more filth.

Williamsburg, our current Brooklyn neighborhood, placed us near a Hasidic community and the company I worked for placed me in the homes of a few modern Orthodox families. The sudden access to a culture known for secrecy quickly turned me into a woman obsessed. These were people previously only discussed in religious schools and seen on Netflix documentaries.

When inside their homes, my brain compiled lists of what I observed as oddities, and I quietly judged much of their lifestyle. I hated how the woman took care of every aspect of domestic life while their husbands were perpetually out. The best a woman could hope for was to be a teacher or someone in the school system where they taught girls who themselves would grow up to be mothers and maybe, if they were lucky, teachers. This cycle seemed maddening.

In my clients' homes, I'd often sneak peeks into the master bedrooms staring at the two full-size beds residing next to one another. I knew the two beds would be there, but it shocked me every time. Sometimes, the beds were separated. Separate beds indicated the woman was on her period or what was culturally known as Niddah or her "unclean" time of month. How confusing, to be deemed impure from a function not only natural, but one whose sole purpose is to bring about new life. This contamination required not only a physical separation from one's husband, but also a trip to the community Mikvah to bathe yourself back to purity once the bleeding resided.

Part of me found the idea of this ritual demeaning, cleaning off something that never needed it, but another part of me couldn't stop fantasizing about it. To be submerged and come out anew was an appealing notion. I wondered if it could really be so easy. I daydreamed about preparing for the Mikvah with the laundry list of requirements:

- Brush and floss teeth
- Rinse mouth well
- Remove nail polish from fingers and hands
- Clean all nails
- Cut all nails
- Remove all jewelry and makeup
- Wash body starting at head and working way down
- Soak body
- Wash hair
- Blow and clean nose
- Clean eyes
- Clean ears
- Clean naval

- Clean vagina internally with warm water
- Comb hair
- Remove contact lenses

At home I completed a google search and found a Mikvah two streets over from my yoga studio. Maybe it was a sign, divine intervention. After a morning vinyasa class, I circled around the block trying to stake out the building and determine what types of women moved in and out of it. It was difficult to ascertain the exact entrance and I never clearly saw any women walking in for the obvious purpose of repurification. With the nerves of calling a new love interest, I dialed and hung up every time the Mikvah receptionist answered. I'd been tempted by artificial fixes my whole life, and after the tenth hang up, I suspected, for the first time, this likely wasn't the answer. Despite being blessed by a rabbi, I knew the water wouldn't save me.

While I didn't feel perfect or holy, I was beginning to come around to the notion I wasn't actually dirty or broken or in a need of cleansing.

I was fine.

My skin was fine. I was safe. I was loved.

Maybe that, with the passing of time, therapy, and self-imposed yoga could be enough?

At class the next morning, I laid on my back staring at the baskets of ferns hanging above me. This was typical of how I spent time before class. Vines connected the individual fern baskets, giving the appearance of plants holding hands. The connecting vines transformed the singular plants into one sizable organism. Perhaps this was supposed to be symbolic of yoga: individuals coming together to form one cohesive entity.

Staring up at the drooping ferns, I wondered who was responsible for watering and trimming them, and if they ever dripped onto the bodies below. Yoga to the People was as obnoxious as the show *Broad City* satirized. A guy unrolled his mat next to me wearing nothing but a pair of boxer briefs small enough to make a European blush. Over the past 12 months, I'd spent more time in close proximity to half-naked men than I had in the last 10 years combined. A young woman to my left rolled out her mat and arranged a collection of amethyst crystals into a shape that wasn't quite a pentagram. Watching her line up the purple stones and snap her hair into a perfect Ariana Grande ponytail aged me half a decade and gave me a better understanding of why people are always hating on millennials. Knowing I left my collection of crystals at home on my dresser, like a decent human, brought about a sense of superiority.

As Brooklynites continued filling the room, I curled up into a tight child's pose with my legs pressed together and my arms flat next to my body. In a seed position, I closed my eyes and pulled in a deep breath through my nose. I tried to focus on feeling present inside my body, like our teachers were constantly instructing, but it had been a long uncomfortable task. My skin hadn't felt like home since I was a kid standing on the pool deck before swim practice, unabashed and feeling powerful. I'd long lived at a distance from my skin. My own racing pulse or the press of another person pushing past me sent distress signals out like sirens punching out from my core. I was determined to not live with my own bodily impulses as triggers. Creating the distance was necessary before, but I was ready to attempt to live differently. I was tired and wanted more for myself. Thirty was a few years ahead, and I wanted to start the decade moving towards the self-assured woman I dreamed of being as a girl.

I closed my eyes and tried attending to the island that was my mat. Taking a deep breath, I attempted to be present in my skin, feel rooted through my body, and melt into the floor. "The mat will hold you," I said, evicting all the air from my lungs. I wanted to believe it. Being held was an intoxicating notion I had trouble trusting. "The mat will hold you," I said again to myself, trying to sink a little deeper into my skin. As over the top as the studio was and how much I hated hipster yogi culture, it felt like something about just "showing up" was working. Slowly, I started to reenter my skin. On my own without magic pills or blessed water.

I started to allow myself to take my pain and my experiences as they were, without the external contexts of

*it wasn't that bad*

*or she had it worse*

or the loudest thought: *was he trying to help you?*

\*\*\*

I believe in science. I trust professionals. As a licensed professional myself, I rely on research and data. There is no guessing in my field, no making assumptions based on what your eyes alone see. At any moment, I can show you if a student's behavior intervention is working or not. The families I work with are vulnerable, often desperate to help their children, and they are sold snake oils and falsities. Over the years, I've watched as they order raw camel milk and send their children to receive hyperbaric oxygen therapy. There is no hard evidence for these "treatments," but someone told them it could help, and they are willing to try. Results have been mixed from parents, some stating to me they have seen huge decreases in problem behaviors, others not noting much of a change. Personally, I have never seen these so-called panaceas work in an overall sense, but I empathize with their desires. I am protective of these families and their resources, both emotional and financial. Seeing overreaching promises and quick fixes are red flags to me, and I try to get my families to harness a suspect mindset of their own. I want to protect them.

This suspicious way of being bleeds into my personal life. As I've journeyed with my own mental health, I've stuck to the straight and narrow of working with therapists who hold PhDs and seeing psychiatrists for medication management, not even trusting the knowledge of primary care physicians to dole out pills. In my mind, holistic avenues were for desperate hippies. On my own time I pour over research articles and read the latest trends in healing for people who have experienced sexual assault. My brain bursts with facts and figures.

Over the past few years my mind has made great strides with psychotherapy. It no longer acts as my harshest critic; it's calmer, and most days it can differentiate between hyperbolic negative thoughts and reality. For as much growth as my brain has made, my body is far behind. Loud noises and visual stimuli agitate my body. Environmental stress causes my muscles to spasm, my pulse races unexpectedly, and a spot on my back renders numb, tingling for hours on end. My thighs and biceps twitch daily without explanation. My body doesn't listen to me, even when I tell her everything is okay, even when I tell her to relax and reassure her that we're safe.

At times, the agitation pulsing through me feels intense enough to punch a hole through a metal subway pole. Friends and my therapist tell me to investigate body work, but I'm resistant. As a millennial living in Brooklyn, I assume body work is an offshoot of tarot, crystals, and herbs. It is more of a tidy, store-bought aesthetic than a deeply rooted set of practices. I'm searching outside myself because I don't have any cultural healing practices of my own. Nothing was given to me from my mom's Southern Baptist roots, which prefers to sweep trauma and darkness under the rug or wrap it within prayers. Nothing has been passed down from my father's Jewish background, except to hyper focus on positivity. Modern day traumas were viewed as gripes to be swatted away. What could possibly compete with my grandmother's mother being the sole person in her family to survive the Holocaust? I've never been taught to even acknowledge difficult experiences never mind being given structure to process them. While the witchy shops in my neighborhood are entertaining, I don't view them as prescriptive and view everything with a skeptical eye "If this stuff was real there would be research. Scientists love publishing, especially successes!" I tell anyone who will listen.

One afternoon after describing a weeklong muscle spasm in my thigh and tightness in my shoulders that won't unwind, my therapist, who I no longer wanted to fuck, suggested I research myofascial release therapy, noting it is backed by some research and recognizing the building frustration with my body. Myofascial release therapy is a hands-on treatment where a clinician applies direct pressure to the body, releasing tension and restoring motion and decreasing pain and tension.

Without pause, I bucked at the idea. "I can't even get a massage. My whole body tightens. Essentially I spend $200 to lie on a table for 60 minutes with full body muscle contractions wondering if the masseuse is wondering why my body is so tight." Despite my resistance, I researched the treatment further on my own, part of me thinking it looked like hocus pocus, a more professional Reiki, but I kept the option rolling around in the back of my mind. It was clear my body wasn't getting better and I knew the talking alone wasn't helping.

On a particularly agitating night, I was exhausted and feeling futile. As I sat scrolling through Instagram watching my upper thigh twitch, I passed a post from Padma Lakshmi. In it, she was speaking to a group of women at a conference for endometriosis encouraging women to self-advocate for their health. I remembered reading her memoir and her struggle with an unnamed, undiagnosed pain. Five years ago, endometriosis was not a word known to most; medications and treatments didn't flash across TV screens like they do today. For eons, women lived and suffered with this chronic condition. Doctors not knowing how to treat these patients have run the gamut of malpractice from wrongfully doing nothing to using a hysterectomy as a last-ditch treatment option. Women have been made to think they're too sensitive about their periods or that this pain was part of the typical experience of living as a woman.

I love data and research, and yet I'd forgotten this well-documented fact; women's pain has never been taken seriously by medical professionals, therefore not well researched, written about, or funded for treatments. A recent study from 2014 documented that 91% of 2,400 women suffering with chronic pain reported gender bias in their healthcare regarding said pain, and half of the women noted doctors suggested the pain was "in their head."[1]

A week later over cheap beers and under strings of colored lights, I monologued this revelation to Roberta, who was well-versed in tarot, herbs, and other witchy ways of healing. She smiled and reminded me that the witchcraft I scoffed at is the original attempt for women to heal themselves and their communities when they were disregarded by male-dominated industries like medicine and mental health. I sneered but leaned in, listening as she detailed a historical context and dismissal of "female" problems from both the medical and psychological fields. As someone who had long been outspoken about Freud's idiotic and misogynistic theories in my own field, I don't know why the realization that medicine was also built on a similar male-centered model wasn't as clear in my mind. This inability to see the obvious is likely due to growing up assuming white collar professionals knew best and the constant messaging that women were dramatic and emotional. Even many of the women in my life had internalized these messages and made it clear that womanhood was expected to be painful and there wasn't use in complaining. Understanding that considering myself without external harmful cultural noise is a subversive act, a bit of a fuck you, and continues to motivate me. Spite in any form has always pushed me out of my comfort zone.

A week later I called the myofascial therapist. From the refuge of a bodega awning, I stood caught in a summer thunderstorm. I watched as people dodge the storm into subway stations and coffee shops. I was sick of feeling trapped.

"I don't know how much I believe in all of this, but I know talk therapy alone isn't working," I said to the therapist over the phone. The rain clacked on the awning above. Ariana, the therapist, didn't demand my life story or push back on my apprehensions. I appreciated her lack of digging. Three years into consistent psychotherapy I was sick of talking about my feelings and experiences. After my ramble ended, she spoke. "Your body is a tape recorder. All the pain, physical and emotional, you have experienced is inside of you. It will never heal by talking alone," she said in a matter-of-fact tone.

That was it - her entire pitch to me was three short sentences. The line went quiet, and I watched the rain pour down in thick sheets inches away from my face. I believed her - my body spoke this truth to me every day.

I made an appointment attempting to be more open with myself. The morning of our session I recognized a tinge of hope in my steps, but I carried my long-held suspicious eye into her office.

After a quick scan, I determined her office held no evidence of hocus pocus. It was plain, painted with a calming dark yellow, reminiscent of a morning desert sunrise. It was a corner office, and the bright winter light filled the room. She was warm and knowledgeable and didn't try to convince me of anything. In my underwear I laid on top of a padded table, and she put her bare hands on my body pressing into the tight parts starting with my shoulders.

"Let me know if the pressure is too much. It shouldn't hurt," she said. To not hurt as part of my treatment was a novel idea. Most weeks therapy hurt mentally, my body ached sporadically, and I assumed hurt would be a part of my overall treatment. The hour felt professional but intimate. I would have let her touch me all day. She didn't fill the room with typical spa sounds of a crashing waves soundtrack or ask me "how are you feeling?" every five minutes.

"Your body knows what it needs," she said after 10 minutes of silence had passed, "You can move it around in whatever way feels good while I'm working." My body had laid in a mummified position for the entire session. I continued not moving a finger or toe for another five minutes. "I don't know what my body needs," I said.

"Just try. You'll know," she said and pressed her hands into the side of my belly. She never asked or analyzed. At some point she started chattering about her own journey to myofascial, which included an almost fatal car accident that left her unable to move her legs for two years.

"Myofascial is the reason I can walk today," she said,

sounding surprised at her own story. As a skeptic, this rang as a tall tale, but I politely nodded and listened.

"Medicine and psychology have yet to meet formally," she stated in response to my rant about the current professional and cosmic worlds I was stuck between. It was nice to hear her thoughts. Her soft voice filled the quiet space and she occasionally encouraged me to stretch my limbs.

Like the good data collector that I am, I asked about her professional background and patients taking mental notes throughout. By the end of the session, the tunnel of my lower back laid flat. My hips moved in a fuller range and my shoulders had lowered half an inch. I didn't know if this would tamper my agitation or if having hands pushed into my muscles felt good just for the moment. But I decided that morning to be okay with either option. My body deserved to feel good.

Maybe in the next decade my chronic tightness, numb spots, skin that feels like a nerve ending, and muscle twitching will have a name defined by medical doctors. Maybe big pharma will peddle out something for me too. For the moment, taking my body seriously was a step towards something. For the first time I was listening to my body without it needing to meet any man-made diagnostic criteria. I validated myself and my experiences, just by trying.

***

A handful of months into consistent caretaking I

met Roberta for drinks. I felt confident that I could drink without self-destruction.

"I am so bored being well," I complained to her inside a bar that smelled reminiscent of my old life, stale beer and disappointment.

"It's the worst," she said, understanding the push and pull feelings.

We mused over our past six months, in which both of us seemed to be healing and doing the strangest thing: not treating ourselves like shit on a regular basis. Over two or three drinks instead of six or eight we conferred about the monotony of it all. I even made sure the beer I ordered didn't have an alcohol percentage over six. Accidently being too drunk was not a risk I could afford. It wasn't a joint effort to stop our old ways; we both just happened to hit our own bottoms around a similar timeline and decided we didn't want to go into our 30s with the pain of our 20s. I was glad we were growing together; it would have been easy to drift apart otherwise. To be off the emotional roller coaster was great, 90% of the time. I liked knowing I was in control of my actions, even if my thoughts jumped around from bad to worse.

I liked knowing that for the first time Alissa could trust me and our relationship. It felt good to be someone she could finally depend on; she deserved it. But self-care for me isn't bubble baths and ordering pizzas. It hasn't been getting my nails done or #treatyoself.

For me, self-care is therapy and talking about your feelings.

Self-care is stopping to think before acting on impulse.

Self-care is talking instead of drinking.

Self-care is talking instead of starving yourself or cutting into your skin.

Self-care is therapy.

Self-care is using phrases like, "I feel ___ and I need ___."

Self-care is changing your negative thoughts into neutral or positive ones; it's learning to sit with hard feelings without reaching for something external.

Self-care is therapy.

Self-care is using phrases like, "When you say ___, it makes me feel ___."

Self-care is giving yourself a break.

Self-care is going to yoga even though you don't feel like it.

Self-care is allowing intrusive thoughts to float by without interacting with them. It's not being mad at yourself for still having intrusive thoughts even though you think you shouldn't be having them anymore. Self-care is using phrases like, "No."

Self-care is therapy.

Self-care is talking about your feelings instead of drinking them.

Self-care is calling your mom more and telling her how you are feeling without worrying about her feelings.

Self-care is talking about your feelings instead of counting out one serving of almonds.

Self-care is accepting that you need to take Valium before bed. It's reminding yourself that taking Valium doesn't mean you're forever broken.

Self-care is not lying to your therapist. It's not lying to

your friends.

Self-care is showing up for therapy even though you'd rather bail.

Self-care is using phrases like, "I can't _____, but I wonder if there is another way I can support you."

Self-care is taking responsibility for your actions. Self-care is reconnecting with your intuition.

Self-care is therapy. Self-care is learning to live in the middle emotionally.

Self-care is boring.

Self-care makes me worry I'll never have anything worth writing about again.

Self-care makes me worry my authentic identity is dull. Self-care makes me feel old.

Self-care has made day-to-day life manageable. Self-care has allowed me to be present and feel connected to others.

Self-care has made me feel so much less alone.

Self-care makes me miss my self-destructive impulses like an old lover. Self-destructive thoughts still knock my skull and whisper into my ear, promising me I'll feel better if I touch them.

I miss them.

I don't actively love my body or think it's a temple, but I've learned that's not an excuse to treat it like trash. That part is hard in our current culture of body positivity. It feels anti-feminist to admit you don't worship your body or aren't striving for radical acceptance of your shape. I still wish to be smaller and to see less of myself, but I don't actively do anything with these thoughts.

Self-care mostly looks like doing nothing when you used to do a lot of somethings.

Self-care is the art of standing still.

Roberta and I transformed our "burn it down" team into a safety club. Now, she channels her negative feelings into tarot and other witchy activities. A few mornings a week I stir a mystery potion Roberta has created for me into my coffee assuming it will conjure self-love, like the bottle she has so carefully crafted. She came out with a line of drops to add to drinks that do an array of things according to plant-based alchemy, and as a skeptic I don't want to believe her, but she seems better so I think she could be onto something.

Sometimes we muse over the parts of the past that felt good.

Roberta and I reminisce about days of blacking out and think about the moment in those nights when everything felt right. We'll always have the memories. I've found the control I've been looking for - spoiler alert, it's me - and I've had it the whole time. I'm creative - I'll find a less destructive chaos elsewhere.

I still love how stale beer smells soaked into wooden bar floors. I no longer use these locations for obliterating myself under the false pretense of being social. I now use these spots for their god intended use of musing and kvetching with friends. Roberta and I talk about our past like we're gossiping about women we used to know and are horrified by, although we long for parts of them and their chaos. Roberta attempts to convince me we can use that "burn it down" energy for a higher purpose than harming ourselves.

"We're meant for bigger things," she says.

# Part II:
## Girlhood

# When We Believed

I entered Monica's room to the sight of her smashing Barbie and Ken's plastic genderless bodies against each other. She sat on her knees and held Barbie and Ken high above their Malibu trailer as she crashed their bodies into each other over and over and over. Hearing the clacking of plastic doll bodies sent a sigh of relief through me. My mom had dropped me off at Monica's house that Saturday morning in second grade the way adults do everything when you're in second grade, without asking. I'd never been to Monica's and new friends' houses made me nervous. At breakfast I picked at my cream-of-wheat with a sick stomach not knowing what smells to expect and worried Monica's mom would offer me a snack I didn't like. As a compliant child, I already knew if offered, I would accept the foul snack and gag it down with a wide grin minding my *pleases* and *thank yous*.

"Hey girly," Monica said as I stood in the doorway. She stopped the fornication and dangled a Skipper doll out for me to take. I maneuvered through the carefully crafted Barbie town. Making my way to Monica, I tiptoed past a laundromat from the 1970s, a RV trailer, a pink Corvette missing one side mirror, a miniature blow-up couch, and a pink and white dream house complete with Tanner, the golden retriever, who stood proudly out front. I took Skipper and found Tommy, Ken's younger brother, in a basket of unchosen dolls. For the rest of the afternoon, Monica and I sat side by side, smashing naked dolls.

Monica's house smelled like vanilla candles and chicken

noodle soup. Her cabinets were full of top-tier snacks and full calorie two liter sodas were always stocked in the fridge. Within one afternoon, this would become my second home. For the duration of girlhood, Monica and I were inseparable. We forced our parents to carpool everywhere, joined the same Girl Scout troop, and rotated houses every other weekend for sleepovers.

It was a late summer weekend right before eighth grade when Monica and I discovered that we possessed supernatural powers. Some might say it was the day we discovered we were witches, although as a good Greek Orthodox, this is not something Monica would say. On this August afternoon we had an entire unsupervised afternoon to fill. Over our post-breakfast phone call, we planned the day.

"Hey girly! Derek told me his family is out of town this weekend. I think we should go over there and take his paddleboat out for a spin around the lake," Monica said. Derek was Monica's new boyfriend and an impressive catch. He was first-string popular and looked like a cliché of a hot California surfer. Like a tall, blonde string bean he towered over most of the boys in our grade. His shaggy hair and dopey puppydog eyes gave him exotic appeal in our preppy East Coast bubble. In between classes he lingered in the hallway flirting with the girls a year ahead of us or joking with a teacher. His signature long hair chronically hung over his eyes, causing him to jerk his head to the left every 30-60 seconds with tic-like precision. I found it distracting, but most of the girls in our grade thought it was *so cute*. In our middle school, Derek was the designated class clown who got away with more than most due to his charm.

\*\*\*

"Hey girly," Monica said, picking up the phone on the second ring. At the time of this call, we're over 20 years out from playing with naked Barbie dolls and from finding out we're supernatural. This is the first time I'd heard her voice in almost a year. It was early in the pandemic and I was seeking out the comforts in all forms. Hearing her animated and bouncy voice was instantly soothing. After college we both left Virginia for various northern states. Our lives now paralleled as newly married people with full-time jobs and babies. Even though I called her on a Saturday, neither one of us had a long, lazy day ahead of us.

"Hey there! Do you remember what happened that day we took Derek's boat out?" I asked as I pushed my 11-month-old through our rapidly collapsing Brooklyn neighborhood. I counted three "NYC strong" signs and four others that read "closed for *now*." The street was emptier than I'd ever seen it. The COVID exodus had started. None of us were wearing masks as currently recommended by the CDC.

"Ohmygod! I haven't thought about that day in so long," Monica said. I heard the click of a stove turning on and her daughter squawking in the background.

"Derek was *so* cool!" I said with a long-forgotten sting of jealousy. "Popular guys never liked me. I was so weird!"

"Guys always liked you," I whined. She exhaled a deep, "whatever," but I could hear her smiling and rolling her eyes. We both know it's true. It was also a fact, men - full-grown men - always drooled over Monica, even when we were tweens. I watched neighborhood dads hang out of their car windows honking and waving. Monica carried an air of confidence. On more than one occasion I saw her tell full-grown high school boys to "sit on it and rotate." She made mixed drinks like a professional by age fourteen and introduced me to every important sexy rated R movie, most notably: *Cruel Intentions*, *The Faculty*, and *Fear*. Hanging out with Monica felt like what I hoped being a grown woman would be.

The morning of the paddleboat excursion we met on the red bridge, which is the halfway point between our houses. The bridge was painted rust red and spanned twenty feet across a small man-made pond. The morning before I learned that I was a witch, I leaned against the already hot metal, waiting, and looking down into the water below searching for signs of aquatic life. Some days I'd walk over the bridge and continue onto the road that led to Monica's house, but that morning I waited in our designated spot overcome by humidity to move further than needed. A few minutes after I arrived, I saw Monica bounding the corner and although she stood a full ten feet away and the air was polluted with the sounds of cars whizzing by, she waved at me and started talking. I could hardly hear her, but it didn't matter, she was on a roll. Monica talked more than any other human I'd ever met. You can ask any teacher, preacher, Girl Scout leader, swim coach, neighborhood child, or haggard mom from Richmond, Virginia and they will tell you she was a big talker. My mouth hadn't yet opened as we headed back to my house, and she rattled off our to-do list:

First, we'd make lizards out of beads and string, which was our first business venture. We sold the hideous creatures for two dollars a pop (until a teacher found a box of cash stuffed in the back of my desk and promptly made us put our enterprise on hold indefinitely).

Second, we needed to sort out the Warhead candy bag my mom bought us from Costco, create a flavor sheet, and then sell the candies (another business which will be thwarted by adults).

Finally, she stated we would walk to the lake to take Derek's paddleboat out for a well-deserved ride.

I know it was Saturday because my mom wasn't home, leaving my dad "in charge." For reasons unknown, he had explicitly instructed us that afternoon not to go to the lake, but I knew he'd be napping between noon and 2 PM. In his parenting career he had never followed through with a demand or given a consequence that carried weight, so it seemed like an easy request to walk around. I also reasoned it sounded like something my mom had told him to say.

"We're going on a walk after lunch," I shouted to him between handfuls of wavy chips and gulps of Sunkist. I licked the salt from my fingers feeling nothing about lying to my dad's face.

We headed to Derek's neighborhood which began where my backyard ended. The invisible line of demarcation denoted a whole new world. When my parents bought our house seven years prior my subdivision was the newest, but now an entire community, bigger and shinier popped up behind us. New neighborhoods seemed to appear every few months in our growing community of elite public schools and helicopter parents. It was the peak of the early aughts. Paris Hilton wore her infamous *Stop Being Poor* T-shirt and families maxed out credit cards and took overreaching mortgages to prove their materialistic American dreams. This notion was most obvious in Derek's neighborhood of Walton Park. Even the mailboxes in Walton Park were comically large. As a young girl I cringed from secondhand embarrassment seeing them; this was pre-Amazon, so it was a grotesque display of McMansions, knowing nothing would wind up in the mailboxes larger than a Sears Catalog.

Pieces of the Walton Park were still in early construction leaving Monica and I to spend many weekends loitering inside the frames of homes-to-be kicking over beer cans to see if leftover beer or piss spilled out. After lunch we passed the wooden outlines of almost-homes and headed straight to the spillway. The spillway was the section of a man-made lake that literally spilled over into a cement rectangle that then narrowed and spilled off again into a creek. Depending on weather and season, it contained zero to three inches of water. Scents of goose shit were ever present, and a thick layer of live algae made parts of the spillway impossible to walk over without slipping. Despite the stink and mud and danger, the spillway was the place many of us had our first kisses and sips of alcohol.

Derek was not only a total fox, but his house sat on the lake connected to our sacred spillway spot. We rang the doorbell and waited. Not a pacing foot or human stirring of any kind came from inside the dark house. It seemed empty. Content, we walked around to the back of his house and

Dyke Delusions

spotted our prize.

On a dad-made beach sat the sky blue, two-seater, pedal boat. Pacing around the vehicle Monica and I eyed one another, hyping each other about our impending theft.

"I'm sure we can take it out. He is my boyfriend after all?" Monica said, inflecting a question at the end of her sentence.

"Of course, I'm sure he'd want you to," I said. This was a bold assumption as Derek and Monica spoke on the phone maybe four times in total and always with their friends hollering and whispering in the background. Boyfriend-girlfriend meant nothing more than staggering together in the hallway at the end of the day and slow dancing under basketball hoops during school dances. I wasn't sure they had even completed those rites of passage yet. Apprehension be damned, without further discussion we pushed and shoved in a joint effort maneuvering the heavy boat into the water where it suddenly became weightless.

"It's not like we're stealing it," I said, pushing myself up and tumbling inside. Monica gave the boat one more shove before getting in herself.

Some pedaling later, we made it out past the shoreline. I dipped my legs overboard to cool off and Monica pulled up her shirt and laid back to tan. For a few moments we sat, letting the breeze push us.

"Where are three places that you'd want to have sex at camp?" Monica sat up and asked.

"I don't know, camp is so dirty," I said, mulling over the question. At this point I'd only tongue kissed one boy for less than 60 seconds.

"I'd want to do *it* in a canoe. Seems romantic to be on the water," Monica said before I could come up with an answer. She'd already been fingered, twice, so I nodded and believed her sexual wisdom. A group of high school boys slugged by wearing backpacks, likely full of beers, and headed down a side path into the woods.

"Hey boys!" Monica stood up and screamed in their direction. The boat rocked and I pulled her back down. I leaned over the boat's side, let out a whistle, and waved. One of the boys sent back a "what's up?" and the other gave us an approving head nod.

Water splashed upwards as Monica stomped her feet in a fit of laughter. Her eyes bugged out at the unwelcome wetness.

"There is a goddamn hole!" she screamed looking down. "How did we not see a goddamn hole!" By this point, our borrowed vessel had floated itself out into the middle of the lake. Within moments water swelled up, soaking our ankles.

"What the fuck do we do?" Monica yelled. I flung my eyes around the perimeter of the lake checking for anyone who could act as a witness to our thievery.

"Well, this is *peachy fucking keen*," Monica said already giving up. "Peachy fucking keen" was her favorite line from the movie *Jawbreaker*. The words left her lips at least 20 times per day, but this utterance made the most sense out of any she ever made.

"Focus, we just have to get the boat back to shore. You're taller, so get in the water and see if you can stand," I instructed.

"Ewww, I can't get into this disgusting water," she said but rolled up her T-shirt, making a crop top, and wiggled out of her shorts, placing them on the top of the boat. "Ugh I'm wearing granny panties today and they're white! What if those guys come back?" she worried aloud.

"Monica, we can't let this boat sink! Fuck those guys!" I said. She jumped in. With a splash her whole body disappeared.

"It's too deep," she said, breaking back up through the water treading in place.

"Try pulling the boat from the front, I'll pedal, and you swim," I instructed. Monica swam the fattest butterfly on her swim team, and she could hold her breath longer than anyone I knew. But the boat was too heavy, it wasn't budging. The water kept rising and now it sat at my calves.

"Get your ass in this lake and help me," Monica demanded. I jumped in with my jean shorts and lime green Limited Too tank top, which frankly I was getting too old to wear. Limited Too had not been considered "in" for at least an entire school year. For the next five minutes we pushed and kicked and kept our heads above water. The boat hadn't budged more than three feet and the shoreline resided an easy 25 feet away from us.

"Fuck, fuck, fuck. We are so fucked," I said now panicked. The boat was halfway beneath the lake. We were losing it to the water. With strong and frantic movements, we attempted to splash the lake water out of the boat. Cupping, throwing, and smacking it out, all while treading water.

"Derek is going to break up with me!" Monica yelled.

"Derek is not going to break up with you because he cannot know about this, or we are going to be grounded. Forget being dumped," I yelled, spitting out mouthfuls of lake water.

"He knew I wanted to see him today, he'll know," she said.

"He won't know, we never saw him, and you never talked to him. Keep pulling," I said, trying to keep the boat afloat and not drown. We managed to swim ourselves in a circle.

"We have to leave it. If someone sees us with it we'll be totally fucked," I yelled. We let the boat go.

Not looking back, we swam away from the sinking vessel and towards the shore.

"Fucking shit, gross!" I screamed while paddling through an algae patch.

Monica tried to hold her shorts up as she swam, but by the time we got out, everything was drenched. "How are we going to explain being soaked and smelling like the goddamn lake?" I asked, standing on the edge looking out as the last corner of the boat was swallowed below the water. Within moments the lake stood still with no signs of its prior destruction.

"We need a fucking miracle, a storm would be great about now," Monica said stepping into her soaked shorts.

We waved and smiled at an older couple who walked past us, their mouths agape. "A great day for a swim," Monica said to their confused faces.

"Maybe we can dry off a little," I said walking over to the grassy field. I lay down, hoping the heat would evaporate the pounds of water soaked into my clothes.

Monica laid out next to me and sent up a faux prayer. "Dear Jesus, please don't let us get grounded and don't let Derek break up with me."

"Amen," I said back, appreciating her efforts.

"That cloud looks like a dog, don't you think? A dog with a big dick," Monica said.

"You're disgusting," I said laughing although I saw what she meant in the amorphous shape.

"Let's go, we'll never dry," I said standing over Monica tugging her body upwards. In my memory I see the clouds, white, puffy, and perfectly shaped like a variety of animals and objects, which can't possibly be true. But Monica too recalls the clouds. I wonder if two people remembering makes a memory true.

A high pitched wail emerged from my son, pulling me out of the past memory Monica and I were talking through.

"Hold on, Monica," I dug through a diaper bag finding a package of teething crackers. "Here buddy," I cooed, hoping this would keep him happy and quiet so I wouldn't have to hang up on my friend who I only spoke to a few times a year.

"Ok, he's good. I'm back," I said into the phone. I heard Monica clank a metal spoon inside a pot and mutter a sweet something at her daughter.

"I can't believe we're moms!" I screamed at the absurdity.

"I know, it's crazy!" she laughed.

"And then it happened, right? My memory didn't make it up, tell me you remember too!" I asked Monica, not giving away my version of the ending, wanting our experiences to match.

"Yes, the goddamn sky cracked with thunder and out poured a summer storm," Monica finished the story which matched the one in my mind.

"We did that, right? Don't you think? Like, we prayed for rain, and it happened. We conjured it up." I said feeling the almost forgotten electric buzz of girlhood.

"I think so, it's so unbelievable. I wouldn't believe it if you didn't remember too," she said as a confession.

"Teen girls are really powerful," I said, turning back onto my block realizing my kid had fallen asleep in the stroller. A couple with packed suitcases passed me in the lobby and a new note on the elevator read: one person or family unit at a time. "Ok well, I'm back home. I have to put this guy down for a nap."

"Me too. I miss you."

"I miss you too."

"Bye girly." I walked back into our apartment trying to remind myself we were still the same powerful girls.

## An Unlikely Shero (On How *Jawbreaker* Helped Me Get My First Kiss)

When I hear people describe themselves as children, I often hear words like *confident*, *silly*, and *happy*. Some of the first words I think of when reminiscing about my childhood self are horny, perverted and curious. Odd and eclectic also come to mind.

I was an elementary schooler who wore two different colored, but coordinating, socks. I kept my old baby teeth in a plastic treasure box and on occasion would take them out to sniff. Once in second grade I orchestrated a fake screaming match with my best friend so we could skip social studies and hang out with our guidance counselor.

For a period in my tweens, I was a serial flasher. I exposed my flat chest to countless neighbors during post dinner walks with my parents and stood on top of hills yanking up my shirt to unsuspecting gardeners as they drove lawn mowers over endless soccer fields. Early on I recognized my interest in observing atypical social interactions.

Despite my antics I was inhibited around my peers. While I was never a bonafide loser, I lived on the outskirts of the popular kids. My fear of rejection exacerbated in seventh grade after I was catfished by a gaggle of popular guys via AIM. Since the incident, I'd been wary of any guy who said he liked me, anxious that I was part of another cruel joke.

But by the end of seventh grade, it seemed like everyone around me was getting their first kiss, with tongue, and I wanted in. More than anything, I wanted my first kiss to be with Troy Williams, but I didn't know where to begin.

Troy Williams was a rich private school boy in our neighborhood of public school kids. He wore exclusively Polo Ralph Lauren collared sheets, had Zac Efron shagged hair, and puppy dog brown eyes. I met Troy at a church youth group meeting that I had been invited to by a neighborhood friend. Due to the number of social groups attached to Christianity, I was in a phase of disavowing Judaism. No one batted an eye to this constant religious and social pairing in our suburb, which was located twenty minutes outside of Richmond, Virginia…the capital of the confederacy, a fact that many of my public school teachers said with pride. Christian youth groups were where all the cool kids hung out, so it was easy to turn my back away from my lineage in order to try and hook a boyfriend. The only hitch was that every time I was around Troy, I was unable to speak. The summer before eighth grade, I vowed to get kissed and gain some confidence before the new school year. It felt like eighth grade would be a make-it-or-break-it kind of year and I didn't want to be left behind.

At our neighborhood pool, I tried creating forward momentum. On a lazy afternoon I met up with Troy and his friends, where I mostly smiled without my teeth while they talked and laughed at their jokes. I chuckled along, although I don't remember if I thought they were funny. During *Adult Swim*, Troy asked if he could get me an ice pop, but when I tried to answer my mouth went dry and I was silent. Unable to regain any control over my vocal chords, I turned around, grabbed my things, and shuffled home in a wet swimsuit. The summer clock was running out of time, and it felt like I had blown my chance.

Back home, I called my friend Monica to report my failure. She suggested a sleepover to cheer me up and told me that boys were stupid and not to worry, that he probably hadn't even noticed. Monica had an older brother, which made her appear chic and worldly. She was always light years ahead of me in popular movies, TV shows, and music. When I arrived at her house that night, we made a list, which we hoped would be enough activities to keep us up all night. Our list that evening included: Mancala tournament, Super Mario World, Kitchen Experiments, Snacks, and to watch as many Rated R movies as we could. Regardless of our lengthy to-do list, it never worked because Monica routinely passed out at midnight. My eyes never shut before three AM There is a saying that if you were asleep last at a sleepover, you're now gay. This tracks for me, and I think it has to do with gay kids radiating social anxiety.

"I have the funniest movie to show you," Monica said as settled into our living room fort with cheeseballs and Oreos at the ready. "It's called *Jawbreaker*, like the candy," she said as the opening credits rolled. The movie opens in the opulent and colorful world of late 90's California. The three most popular girls at Reagan High school kidnapped their best friend for her 18th birthday. Courtney is the ruthless and confident leader of the group. She is played by Rose McGowan at her peak. All the girls wear skin tight dresses and micro minis and six-inch heels. Everything on screen looks like candy, which I guess is the juxtaposition to the film's dark actions. When the girls arrive at the Waffle House and pop the trunk, their friend is blue and stiff and dead. Courtney casually mentions that she jammed an entire jawbreaker in Liz's throat.

The costumes are amazing, the soundtrack is insane, and the dialogue is perfect. "Ok, reality check, Liz is in the trunk of this car. And she is dead. That is a sad, fucked up thing, but you are going to walk into that school and strut your shit down the hallway like everything is peachy fucking keen."[1] As I watched, mouth agape and eyes glued, I could feel myself coding the film in my bones. This was a feeling that happened to me, and still does, when I click on a piece of art and I can feel it shaping me or guiding me. I knew within 20 minutes that this film would belong to the canon of films that molded my young personality.

While I was eccentric and horny, I was also deeply insecure. The shock I felt watching Courtney Shayne strut around her school demanding what she wanted and being overtly sexual lit a bulb in my brain. For years, I carried around a sense of otherness I couldn't put my finger on, and it left me feeling socially uncomfortable even around my good friends. I felt that my impulses were sluttier than everyone around me. Sure, my friends wanted to be kissed but I wanted to see what a rock hard dick looked like up close. This was a time when Jessica Simpson and The Jonas Brothers were preaching about saving themselves for marriage and sporting trendy purity rings. Many of my friends fell in line, obsessed with their chastity jewelry and Christian summer camps. It wasn't easy for a closeted lesbian, sex-curious Jewish kid in the South. I did what I had to do to conform - which was mostly keep my mouth shut.

*Jawbreaker* showed me sexually confident women. It brought to light ideas about kink, pleasure, and power in a way I had never seen before. Courtney was never ashamed or punished for her sexuality. If anything, her games make her boyfriend more obsessed. In one scene she instructs him to lick and suck on a bright orange popsicle as if it's a dick, her dick: "suck my big stick." She then gets him to blow a popsicle while she goes down on him, briefly as the cops interrupt. Sexuality is played with in the movie in a way that came off as playful, not stigmatizing.

Unlike other antiheroes of the time, Courtney didn't talk to herself in a way that was disparaging towards her body. Sure, she engaged in deeply immoral actions: a one-night stand with a man to get him accused of a rape that he didn't commit, blackmail, and killing her best friend with little to no remorse ("I killed the teen dream, deal with it") just to list a few. I'm not implying she was the moral compass of my youth, not that I was looking for one, but she did instill in me a sense of sexual power that was self-serving. Courtney also gives us one of the best and underutilized phrases from film history: *peachy fucking keen*. This is a phrase Monica and I would say no less than one hundred times a day at the height of our *Jawbreaker* mania.

During a time when most female protagonists were relaying messages of self-doubt and low self-esteem, Courtney Shayne was out here organizing murder cover-ups and playing kinky sex games with her boyfriend without breaking a sweat or worrying over other people's opinions of her. This is a woman who knows exactly how to play every situation, obviously until the end where everything unravels and she does go to jail, but the last 60 seconds aside.

With a few weeks left of summer and nothing to lose, I tested out my Courtney Shayne alter ego. Over AIM I threw being coquettish out the window in lieu of going full blown whore. With Troy I was finally bold.

*Shimmynshke: Anna told me you thought I was hot.*
*TroyDawg06: You already knew that*
*Shimmyshke: so what are you going to do about it?*
*TroyDawg06: …..*
*Shimmynshke: ….? I thought you'd hooked up lots of girls before…but maybe Anna was lying. Sorry, nevermind I guess*
*TroyDawg06: I have. Let's meet at the spillway*
*Shimmynshke: Are you sure? Its no big deal if you don't want to*
*TroyDawg06: See you in 20*

I brushed my teeth and dabbed my mom's Clinique Happy perfume onto my wrists. I put on the only bra I own. It was a cotton training bra that I didn't need, but I wanted him to see the straps poking out from under my tank top. Troy was already at the spillway when I arrived via a teal Trek mountain bike.. The spillway was the concrete part of the man-made lake in our neighborhoods where the water literally spilled over. Most days it didn't have more than a few inches of water sitting in it. In the summer, sun-baked algae pieces scattered along the bottom. Geese milled about pecking and pooping. It was where teens went to make out, smoke menthols, and drink wine coolers. Troy was using the spillway to practice skateboard tricks. I think he was trying to impress me, but he couldn't even land an ollie. Nevertheless, I was turned on.

Sweat rolled down Troy's zit-filled face. The sun beat off his pimples, making them look like tiny red ants crawling along his cheeks and chin.

"Are you going to kiss me or what?" I shouted across the sun-soaked lawn. Goose shit was scattered throughout the area like inescapable mines. Troy dodged dookies on his walk over to me. His board rolled down the cement ramp, hitting a pile of stones at the bottom. He stood in front of me with his helmet still on, unclipped, the way all the skater bois wore it. Watching the clips swing under his chin made me even hornier. My insides felt like they were melting, but I visualized Courtney Shayne in her silk nighty and pigtails bossing around her boyfriend. I took his helmet off and tossed it on the grass.

Troy put his hands on my waist and stepped closer. One of his zits was so white, I feared it would burst at any moment.

"Wait! We both have braces," I said, tapping my teeth, worried we would be locked together. I visualized my mom driving us to the orthodontist to be forcibly unhinged.

He laughed, "Braces don't really stick together from kissing." I licked my tongue over my metal railroad tracks and hoped he was right.

"Close your eyes," he said.

I snapped them shut just as he pressed his mouth

against mine. I was kissing a gorgeous, popular boy, and he was shoving his tongue into my mouth. I had done it. It felt slimy and wonderful, even though I wouldn't get my period for another four years, this moment was my transformation into womanhood.

"How was it?" he asked, pulling back after less than fifteen seconds.

"Peachy fucking keen," I said. I handed him back his helmet and sat on the edge on the lawn surrounded by goose shit. For the rest of the afternoon, I watched as he never landed an ollie.

# Camp Out

As a hungover human, arriving at work by 7:45 AM to a group of roaring teens bordered on impossible. On the McDonald's breakfast menu, I found solace. In the parking lot of the YMCA, I filled up on hash browns layered in ketchup, which in combination with black coffee acted as a cure-all for my sour stomach. By 10:00 AM, the amalgamation of McDonald's and warm sun expelled the hangover from me. The bounce back of young bodies is extraordinary.

After my first year of college I needed a job with similar routines to campus life: work time, play time, sleep time. The summer day camp schedule afforded me the ability to drink too much at night, spend my days tanning, and dodge my attraction to women by surrounding myself with young attractive men to flirt with. Summer camp was a wholesome place to hide.

On the first day of training, a seasoned counselor advised me to work with the younger campers warning me about the teen group. "They're hellish. Coed adolescents are all catfights and romantic dramas." he said.

The pushy veteran continued: "You look like you could be a teen camper yourself. Those teen girls are mean, they will eat you alive. I saw one of them call Marcus a faggot last summer. He cried in the pool shed for the rest of the afternoon. She was forced to write him an apology note, but no one looked at her twice afterwards."

I hadn't formally met any of the counselors and was curious about the reasoning behind this unsolicited advice.

When the time came to rank our top three desired job positions, I wrote the teen group in the number one spot on my list. I didn't like being told I couldn't excel at something. It also comforted me to know the teens could swim, feed themselves, and ask for help if needed. The thought of standing around a crowded pool watching fifteen 5-year old children swim drowned me with anxiety. I was not looking to be particularly responsible over the next 12 weeks.

Teen Extreme, the painfully accurate name of the teen camp group, consisted of thirty coed, 12 to 16 years old, with three regular counselors and one camp director who was my reported boss. Reported Boss was a laid-back, late twenty-something male who was easy to please. All I had to do was not to lose anyone on a field trip or not bring anyone back from archery bleeding and he acted as if I taught them Mandarin. On the first day of camp, I established my authority amongst the teens by "accidentally" saying *fuck* and teasing the most popular teen boy.

The other female counselor was Hannah, a devoted Christian woman who belonged to one of big new age churches in our town. She earnestly spoke about the power of god's will and the everyday usefulness of prayer. Other counselors scoffed when she declared one day, she would open an orphanage and school in Haiti (which she later did and continues today). Even though Hannah knew I was mostly a drunk Jewish slut, we bonded and spent our days laughing and making fun of our campers. Throughout the summer she acted as a surprisingly nonjudgmental rock to lean on. A lightness emanated from her. A warmth touched everyone she encountered. Even as a sarcastic and suspiciously secular person, I found myself believing in the power of her prayers by watching the way in which her life unfolded and the positivity that buoyed her through the day. It was hard not to be a little bit in love with her. She was affectionate, often touching my back or leg and hugging me hello every morning. An unwanted spark brewed inside my guts. I wanted her attention. These feelings towards women were familiar. I'd harbored them to some degree since elementary school, but since I'd allowed myself to start kissing girls under the guise of drunken antics at college, the feelings were becoming harder to ignore.

On the rare occasion she came out to a party, Hannah would nurse one drink for over an hour, and I hoped in her altered state she would keep her hand on my knee for a second too long or hold eye contact for a length of time considered as flirting. It never happened. She spent most of time recalling mistakes of her past such as the one instance of premarital sex or drinking past the point of intoxication. At first, it felt like she wanted to guide me towards a happier way of being. She made me feel like the most important person in a room, and everything I said seemed meaningful to her. The sense of specialness she cultivated in me was intoxicating.

Then one night before dinner she convinced me that we should check out a quick service at her church. If she asked me to fly to Haiti that night I would have said yes. Inside a church the size of a football field, I sat amongst the adults and children standing with their hands up in the sky in worship and watched wide-eyed as many of them burst into tears moved by this higher power. Hannah swept tears from her eyes and held my hand. No tears formed in my eyes. For the first time, Hannah's hand in mine didn't feel like magic. I realized Hannah was trying to start the conversion process with me. I thought back to our conversation and realized she had told me in various ways she was a missionary. She was dazzling and I felt safe around her, but I began wondering whether she liked me as a friend or saw me as a summer project. Having already tried out Catholicism in the sixth grade, six months before my Bat Mitzvah, I was not in the market for conversion.

Marcus rounded out our counselor group as a mid 20's objectively handsome hyper-athletic type. I instantly took up flirting with him feeling like it was the most sensible thing to do. Reported Boss, Hannah, Marcus, and I functioned as a mismatched but harmoniously running team.

My team and the higher-ups at the camp were surprised at how well I managed the teens, especially seeing as I stood 5 foot 3 inches and was hardly 19. I didn't look much older than most of the kids and blended into the group when we walked as a pack crossing the sports field. The majority of our campers were typical suburban kids around 12 and 13, but we also housed a handful of 15 and 16 year olds, most of whom didn't want to be there but whose parents didn't trust them to stay at home alone all day.

The most troublesome of these misfits was Nia who was angst-filled and openly gay. Two mornings a week she attended her church's sexuality conversion classes. Our camp didn't condone these types of treatments, but it happened off campus, so we didn't have much of a say in the matter. On those days Nia would arrive back to camp post lunch. My heart broke for her, but I dreaded hearing the walkie talkie announcing her return on those days:

Office: *Office to Teen Extreme. Nia K. drop off. Headed to picnic tables. Copy.*

Sam: *Sam to office. Waiting. I see her. She's heading over. Copy.*

"Did you fuckers miss me?" Nia swaggered under the pavilion and dropped her bags.

"Nia. Language." I said.

She took out her lunch, walked over to the girls' table, and shoved Megan, a popular girl with barely-there jean shorts and smudged eyeliner.

"Nia, that's enough. Last warning or you're going back to the office." I said.

"She knows this is my seat." Nia whined. I pinched the back of my arm underneath the picnic table, the sting allowing me to take a deep breath and squeeze out the agitation.

On another late drop-off day, Nia arrived during afternoon swim time. All the boys and a handful of the girls splashed in the pool playing sharks and minnows. Most of the girls sat out tanning and passing around their headphones. They obsessively shared music the way you did in your youth when songs are the language that explains you the best. Nia passed by everyone and sat on a lounge chair across from me relacing her combat boots.

"I'm sorry you have to go to those classes. I hope you know we all support you here," I said to her in a rare moment of calm between us.

"I don't care about the classes; I just meet other girls.

We all date each other and hook up. It's so stupid for adults to put all the gay kids together in class." She said this with a hard laugh and without a blink of discomfort, her boot laces perfected.

"It must be tough though. To hear the terrible shit they say to you all. To know your parents want you *converted*. I'm sure that feels awful." I said, trying to give her permission to feel pain.

"It's not. I really don't care." She stood up and walked over to the snack bar. Her absence of shame or at least sense of frustration caused my right eye to twitch. The lack of struggle felt flagrantly disrespectful. This was the jumping off scenario to create a runaway teen or at the very least a girl with serious depression, and yet Nia bounced through the ordeal with a pocketful of phone numbers for prospective dates. Her confident butch edge rattled me, and I oscillated between disliking her, wanting to be her, and hoping to protect her, although she didn't need it. I worried that, without my discipline, I could end up like her. Of course I wanted to talk back and be too loud and boldly flirt with Hannah, but I had self-restraint.

I could hardly fathom the idea of my desires and here was Nia, chasing them openly.

One night after work I stopped off at the public library to check out season four of *The L Word* on DVD. My mind already planned how I could quietly watch it on my laptop at home without anyone knowing. On my way to check out I bumped into Nia. She was walking backwards giggling into her cell phone with a handful of magazines. *Smack*. she stepped on my foot, and I almost put my face in the back of her hair. She turned around, eyed the DVDs, and looked back up at me with a side smile. Despite just spending eight hours together we acted like polite strangers.

My brain bulleted a list:

- *It's for a college summer project*
- *It's for my friend*
- *Watching a show doesn't make you gay!*
- *I meant to grab* Sex and The City*!*
- ~~*I'M SECRETLY A LESBIAN TOO! PLEASE TELL ANYONE*~~
- *You're wrong, it was the* Friends *box set*

I wanted to have excuses at the ready when she brought it up to the whole group the next day. But she stayed silent. Nia never uttered a word about our encounter. She teased me a little less but generally continued acting noncompliant. That summer Katy Perry released her 2008 hit "I Kissed a Girl" and my group of tweens blasted the song daily. After belting out the chorus with her friends, Nia smiled knowingly and asked me if I had ever kissed a girl. I faux scolded her saying she knew it wasn't an appropriate question, but assumed my flushed face gave her the answer. Her bold queerness caused me to be harder on her than the others.

At dusk the campers scattered home picked up by a litany of caregivers and the majority of the counselors would head to someone's house to drink cheap beer and trade stories about the day.

Working with children for eight hours a day always

made for good storytelling. A nine-year-old boy likely transformed his penis into a weapon in the changing hut and a little girl was bound to divulge a family secret (*My daddy lives downstairs in our house*). I drank excessively and flirted with everyone. By the fifth week of camp, I had made out with four of the ten male counselors, and while I might have been developing a bit of reputation, I was relieved it was that I was a slut instead of a dyke.

Towards the end of the summer my feelings for Hannah escalated and in an attempt of transference I ramped my flirting with Marcus. Hannah was leaving for the West Coast and had no plans on returning. I worried I'd miss her in ways I shouldn't. While I aimed to perfect the part of girlfriend to nice boy, Marcus started making overreaching requests like asking if we could go on actual dates and wondering if I could I stop making out with the other counselors at parties. Although I wanted his attention, I knew committing to anything more than base level heterosexual banter would be hard to maintain. My brain constantly churned thinking about how Marissa and Summer of *The O.C.* would behave to better gauge my own behavior; would drinking too much and crying be the move, or should I act cold and distant? I desperately wanted to play the part right, never knowing whom I was trying to convince more.

Knowing I would have to go back to school soon, I decided to fuck Marcus. In my mind this would convince everyone of my straightness and create fodder for my friends back at school. I imagined pretending to miss him and sullenly texting him in front of everyone, stepping out of loud rooms to take his calls, and arranging weekend trips to visit my older boyfriend who I was obviously very attracted to. Marcus and Reported Boss threw a party the weekend of July Fourth. Within an hour I drank approximately half of a keg and ingested an entire baking sheet of Jell-O shots. Hannah stopped by and, in the hopes of making her jealous, I confided in her my feelings about Marcus and how I wanted to sleep with him. She squealed at the idea of two people she loved getting together and told me nothing would make her happier than to see us together.

After she left, I sat alone on a tuft of grass in a warm haze watching counselors dance in the backyard with sparklers. One of the boys fired off a small batch of fireworks. Everyone's skin glistened in the humidity and Marcus settled in next to me on the ground musing about the romance of hot summer nights. He kissed me under the artificially lit sky surrounded by the hissing and crackling of fireworks. A numbness spread from my lips to my tongue and moved throughout my guts, chest, and hands.

I led Marcus to his room where I took off my shirt and his pants. He was too old for his room to be in the shape that it was, smelling like sour socks and musty sheets, likely unchanged since the start of summer. The breaths between kissing tasted like dirt and grass. Three nights a week he played in a coed soccer league.

His body felt like stone. The hardness of male bodies routinely surprised me. I wouldn't make eye contact with him. I tilted my head towards the second-floor window and listened to the murmurs and shouts of the party below. A crackle of a sparkler and the steady plunk of beer pong balls filled the room. Wave after wave of nothing crashed over me as we had sex. His clean-shaven face, smooth and damp, buried in my neck. My body, a shell.

Afterwards he held me. The hair of his armpits dampened my shoulder. I wasn't used to this level of affection from the random boys I fucked back at school. It took all my willpower not to shriek from disgust.

"Stay over tonight. We can go to work together in the morning." He said kissing the back of my neck. Wrapped in his arms my lungs started to collapse. I laid as still as a corpse waiting to hear his breath even out into sleep before I left and hitched a ride back to my house with another counselor.

Marcus brought me a coffee the next morning at work and I watched as he waltzed around all day like a person thinking he was on the edge of something new. After work I met him at his car; we had plans to go meet up with the other counselors. On the drive out he squeezed my thigh and told me he had been thinking all day about the night before. His eyes searched my face for a sign to confirm a mutual feeling. The thought of explaining myself was too exhausting, so I brightened my eyes and smiled. I ran my fingers down his cheek thinking that's what someone in lust would do.

On the second to last Wednesday of camp, an extensive hangover left me tossing and turning. After a night of no sleep, I texted Marcus at 6:30 AM to meet me in the parking lot at work promising coffee and hash browns. Of course he said he would be there without hesitation because he was sweet and great, and I hated that I couldn't just like him. Over a dewy picnic table with a makeshift breakfast,

I rambled an apology stating we needed to just be friends. He acted crushed, moping around the morning. Later he'd oscillate between ignoring me in group settings to drunk-calling me urging me to give our relationship a chance. I didn't like him, but spent the summer playing him hot and cold, enjoying the attention.

Summer camps are like high schools, so news already traveled that Marcus and I had slept together. I assumed everyone thought I was the biggest slut of the summer, but that morning, I felt content to have the sun, my stupid campers, and a bag of hash browns. After that morning, I started distancing myself from Hannah, Marcus, and Reported Boss and began hanging out with the other counselors closer to my age. With space it started to appear that what seemed like a genuine friendship with Hannah had really been her targeting me as a red flag of brokenness for her to convert and fix. It was difficult to tell what parts of our relationship were real.

By the last weekend of the summer, I decided I could go on in this artificially constructed, empty way of drinking, transferring, being touched by a warm body I didn't care about, silencing myself, and lying. I observed the way the other girls talked about Nia behind her back. They called her a dyke and excluded her from weekend gatherings, but worst of all they felt sorry for her. She was out of control and troubled, she would never go anywhere in life. I couldn't stand the idea of pity or, worse, not leading a successful exterior life. My ability to mold into the woman I thought I was supposed to be - straight, thin, and quiet - was the line that separated us. It was a line I thought I could hold.

I decided then that I would commit to molding, no matter the cost. At the time, the synonymous word for molding, *to whittle away*, didn't cross my mind.

# The Great Escape

Moving away from Virginia was a natural knowing. Even as a teen I knew the state I was born in would not be the state I settled. For most of my upbringing I lived feeling like an outsider. Conservative values saturated my public schools and neighbors, seeping out as a clear desire to maintain a traditional status quo (white, hetero, and Christian). In fifth grade my dad drove a van full of us to Cotillion joking that a few decades I wouldn't have been allowed to attend as the country club only recently allowed Jews. I followed his lead and laughed along. Now I wonder why they wanted me to take part in such an archaic and frankly racist activity. Of course, not all of my feelings of otherness are directly correlated to the 10th state to join the union, but it was an easy place to direct my discomfort. Early on I fantasized about the openness and perceived glamor of popular coast towns. Particularly, New York City, which in my mind glowed as the island of misfit toys; a place I might fit in.

The summer after 9/11 my mom, moved by the zeitgeist of patriotism, decided that our family needed to take a four-day trip to New York City. In the oppressive humidity of summer in Virginia, we stood outside the cottage-sized train station waiting for our Amtrak. With five dollars from my dad, I perused the snack bar. To my horror, a stack of homemade ham and cheese sandwiches wrapped in cling wrap and hard boiled eggs were front and center. I settled on peanut M&Ms. A woman wearing a stained baby blue sweatsuit thumbed through a newspaper and coughed at regular intervals. On the train, I listened to the *Thoroughly Modern Milly* and *Rent* soundtracks, flipped through a *Seventeen* magazine, and ignored my family, feeling adult and independent. It was only my second time visiting the city, but Mom recalls how I expertly navigated the subway and didn't seem bothered by the crowds, freaks, or chaos.

Alissa, who had long sworn she would never move to New York City, finally agreed after I threatened a cross-country move to Los Angeles. Graduate school was coming to an end, and I knew this was my time to leave the state I had spent my whole life in. We both knew our relationship wouldn't survive otherwise.

Alissa needed to move to live as her most authentic self, which was proving impossible for her. She had recently outed herself to her family while living and working in the town she grew up in. She was teaching at her own elementary school and the thought of reintroducing herself to her old town was overwhelming.

"Everyone already knows me as this one thing. I don't want to have to come out to everyone," she said, feeling defeated one afternoon. It didn't help that Virginia had no legal protection for LGBTQ employees, and conservative undertones whispered throughout workplaces made those identifying as othered feel less than welcome. People made comments, especially when they didn't know you were *one of them*. As an outwardly femme woman who appeared gender typical, I was privy to such perverse thoughts. My supervisor at my school psychologist internship was a "Christian" woman with a hard-on for family values. Once after a phone call with an upset parent she said to me, "Well that poor girl wouldn't be bullied if her parents didn't let her wear boys' clothes to school and cut her hair like that. It's confusing to the other children."

My stomach knotted as I kept a straight face. I needed her to give me a passing mark for the semester to graduate. Up until this point, she treated me warmly, or the version of me I presented to be, and I didn't want things to change between us. What I thought I wanted was to keep my relationship with this woman as it was - amicable and kind - but I didn't realize that what I was avoiding was being confronted with my own complex feelings about my identity. As a newly out person I still lived in a state of quasi-acceptance. It felt easier to pass and stay quiet than to observe the possible discomfort I might conjure in others.

On July 3, 2013, Alissa and I packed a moving truck and drove from Northern Virginia to New York City to try to see if we could live out of the closet as a couple. Technically, her dad drove the truck to the city, but Alissa drove us in her Nissan Rogue and a trunk full of leftover boxes. We declared July 3rd our own Independence Day.

The summer Alissa and I moved to New York City, I finished graduate school and was itching to *be* someone other than a student. *Be* a real woman, an out girlfriend, and maybe be a lady about town.

I couldn't have consciously thought I would show up to a new city and transform into a new person, leaving my past behind. On some level I knew the idea was magical thinking, a well-played out trope. But despite my smarts, I'd harbored fantastic fantasies about newness; a job, an apartment, hip friends, dark bars, and a new way of being. I fantasized about living as a grown woman with the confidence of a 1,000 dyke camp counselors, a woman whose insides felt secure and calm. Maybe I would stop mulling over sharp objects and ingested carbs. Maybe I could fall asleep without counting and praying. I daydreamed about being with Alissa without her swatting my hand away in public, looking over her shoulder while we were out, and living life where I didn't feel like a secret.

We arrived in the city with one employed person, Alissa, who landed a job as a first-grade teacher at a charter school and $7,000 combined in our savings accounts. At 25, I had never held a full-time job and despite spending the entire spring and early summer seasons trying to secure one, all I had to show was a handful of dead-end interviews.

Our sixth-floor walkup apartment building stood on the gayest intersection in the city, maybe even the whole country, Christopher Street and 7th Avenue. This section of the West Village rivals West Hollywood with its historic landmarks like the The Stonewall Inn, Duplex, and the abundance of leather stores unapologetically selling rubber body suits in their display windows.

The famous bar, Marie's Crisis Café, belted out show - tunes throughout the night and the drag queen dressed as a demented Bea Arthur doing crowd control in front of Big Gay Ice Cream was sure to shade anyone walking past.

Standing on the sidewalk holding a box of kitchen wares, I watched a double decker tour bus circle around Christopher Street Park. The park holds statues of gay and lesbian couples and is popular among tourists and cat-sized rats. I remembered being 14 on top of the same bus with my family feeling my face blush as we rounded the corner and saw the statues. Part of me couldn't believe Alissa and I were here.

A young, fit Russian mover puked on the sidewalk before lifting our armchair out of the back of the moving truck. His pores stunk of rubbing alcohol.

"It's just the heat," he slurred, proceeding to carry the furniture up the four flights of stairs. He dropped the chair in the entryway and excused himself to the bathroom. Sounding like a cat choking up a hairball he puked on and off all afternoon in our only bathroom, attached to our bedroom.

2013 was a scorcher, or maybe all summers are scorchers in the city when you have a mediocre AC window unit. I took two to three body showers per day and went through 20 baby wipes before 5 PM wiping away sweat. Our first summer in the city, I soaked up our new surroundings. I watched Alissa tepid, but intrigued.

We had three weeks to explore Manhattan before Alissa started work. Every morning we woke up and walked downstairs to the Dunkin' Donuts, fueling up on iced coffees before heading out on our daylong walks. We meandered to the Christopher Streets piers, which were more gentrified than the images I had in my mind from watching *Paris is Burning*. In fact, I never saw a sex worker before 11 PM anywhere in the West Village. We ate our way through Chelsea Market and people-watched in Washington Square Park. Almost daily we trekked across town to the East Village to meet up with Lindsay, Alissa's sister. It was a straight shot down 3rd Street passing

Washington Square Park and NYU students covered in purple and silver garb. At least two nights a week, Lindsay brought us to her favorite restaurants where we got drunk on cocktails we couldn't afford.

For our first city date I took Alissa to One Gin, a Russian bar in our neighborhood. The bar known for its homemade flavored vodkas and gothic interior was filled with attractive and well-dressed humans. It felt like a scene from *Eyes Wide Shut*, and I was underdressed in my striped Gap shirt, skinny jeans, and high-top converse. We sat at the bar, and I drank my way through a vodka flight while Alissa sipped a strawberry cooler. Surrounded by twinkling votives and two guys in expensive suits who three minutes earlier asked if we were sisters, we kissed. Our three-year-old relationship had never experienced intimacy outside. Alissa touched my leg and kept her mouth close to mine all night. Her confidence, although bolstered by booze, gave me hope that we might be able to make our relationship work in the real world.

Friday nights after Alissa got off from training at her elementary school, we would have dinner at Waverly Restaurant and catch up on our days. Over chocolate chip pancakes, tuna salad, a combination of French fries and onion rings, and the best ranch dressing north of the Mason-Dixon line, we watched a bold new world go by. Alissa began to settle into her skin watching the eccentricities carrying their heads high outside the diner window. Seeing the kings, queens, and in-betweens of the West Village gave us suburban lesbians the confidence to start doing the same. Waverly Restaurant was the first place in the city that felt like ours. The only thing it lacked was matzah ball soup. It was nice to see Alissa feel more assured about her sexuality and our relationship. For the first time she was making friends as her most authentic self. Every time no one cared about her having a girlfriend, she stood a quarter inch taller.

For a few months it seemed like my magical thinking was working. Our Christopher Street apartment did bring about an escape from my past in the way new stimuli have the ability to do. I was spending my days job hunting and memorizing the city streets with my feet. One afternoon I took my résumé to a restaurant in the village, where the self-appointed restaurant *it* girl (her dad owned the place) glanced down at my qualifications and then back to me, mentioning a dishwasher job was available. Despite having three years' experience as a barista, my incomplete knowledge of latte art and lack of hipster apparel left me short in all the local coffee shops. There could be an entire walking tour of places in the West Village I've interviewed. In November I landed a job at a private school for students diagnosed with autism spectrum disorder. At the school I met a few people who weren't friends but were at least humans to drink with.

I felt better, for a while, but the longer we lived in the city old flashes appeared again, bringing me back to the past. Working in a school setting proved difficult, around every corner were reminders of my childhood. One afternoon in the school library a student brought me a copy of *The Rainbow Fish* and my ears echoed with Nick's voice, "Sam come over, I know this one is your favorite." The sight of grape jelly breaking through white bread automated a lump of vomit in my throat. No matter the city I lived in, the job I worked, the people I met, or the number of overpriced drinks I emptied, my memories kept circulating through my blood and echoing in my brain. I had forgotten about these details, and now they were in my face, forcing me to remember.

# The Keeping and Care of You

As a tween I often spent time topless in front of my bathroom mirror examining my breasts. The urge to study them cropped up unannounced, so most nights I stood half dressed in jeans, pajama bottoms, or sometimes in tights and a pulled down leotard. I'd scrutinize my breasts in contrast to the ones I saw in the pages of my American Girl book, *The Keeping and Care of You*, which was a preteen guide to puberty. The book housed a few pages concerning breast development, and it displayed cartoon pictures of breasts in a variety of shapes and sizes, mostly appearing in that odd in-between phase of growth. The onset of puberty jolted a new awareness about my skin and triggered suspicions about my body. My body seemed to grow and stretch without my consent, and suddenly it no longer felt like a comfortable place to live. Before my pubescent years, I enjoyed existing in my thin and boyish frame. I liked how my flat chest and tight stomach moved through the world. It seemed as if overnight my sharp hips were rounding out and my stomach was softening. But it was my breasts that I struggled with the most. To me, they suggested two red flags denoting to others of my impending sexuality and maturity, neither of which I wanted.

"Where did you get those things?" my mom joked as I stripped off my shirt tossing it into the washing machine one night. At some point during my sophomore year of high school, my breasts had grown larger than hers. "You certainly didn't get those from me!" she laughed. She was right - they weren't hers. My breasts derived from a long line of Sephardic Jewish breasts, which are notoriously oversized and dense. Both my paternal grandmother and paternal aunt had undergone breast reduction surgery, tired of hulling around a pair too large for their frames. While I didn't struggle with size like them, I did belong to the long lineage of women who had complex relationships with their breasts. My mom was able to make this joke just a few years after she had completed chemo and radiation therapies for her own early onset of breast cancer. At the time it felt like the cancer was a breast issue solely belonging to her, which I attributed to bad luck, and maybe it was. At 39, the time of her diagnosis, she was a runner and training to be a fitness instructor; she was the most in-shape she had ever been. None of us could make sense of it. My consideration was for her health and as an arrogant youth, I was able to distance myself from her breasts, and like she said, I didn't get mine from her.

Post high school and college I found ways to cohabitate with my breasts, but I never felt close to them. I hated how they sat too far apart; I can put an entire palm in between them. I wished they were higher, bounced with more perk. But in general, I disconnected myself from them, allowing them to exist on me like barnacles along an ocean pier. The discomfort of puberty had caused me to rebel against my body; I didn't want to live there and felt no need to care for it. I spent the next decade and a half treating it poorly in a variety of ways. Then at 27, when I had almost forgotten about them, something new started happening at my yearly gynecological appointments. Doctors would inquire, as always, about my family's breast health, but now they would say "*soon* you'll have to get a mammogram or a sonogram." Suddenly, I was confronted with my breasts in a way that was harder to ignore, but I managed for a while longer, because *soon* hadn't yet come.

It isn't easy to navigate breast health today; different doctors have told me disparate protocols. Some prescribed a required mammogram 10 years prior to my mom's diagnosis date, others have suggested a sonogram at age 35, and another stated the regular mammogram age of 40 would suffice as the BRCA gene doesn't run in my family. Over this past summer I went to my gynecologist for my yearly pap and breast check. I decided the year prior to settle on a practice I trusted, deciding whatever they said about my breasts I'd listen to because I knew I had to make a choice. If I didn't, I could have stayed going around on the medical merry-go-round for the rest of my life.

"Your breasts feel great," my doctor said as I wrapped up my exposed self in the soft gown waiting for her to tell me what I would need to do within the next 3–5 years. "I want you to go get a sonogram. I'll write you the prescription today. What location is better for you?" she asked, showing me two options.

"Now? I thought I could wait until I was 37, the earliest 35." I said, confused.

"I like my patients to get a baseline 10 years before their mother's diagnosis date, so you're actually 2 years behind my recommendation," she said. "It's just a baseline, so we know what your tissue looks like."

I left lightheaded with the news. My lackluster feelings towards my breasts had been a long-held, guilt-filled secret.

In our culture of body positivity and self-acceptance, I felt shame, like the proverbial bad feminist, for not embracing this acutely female part of myself. I spent the next 30 days ignoring my doctor, thinking about how young 39 was, and feeling disappointed for the years spent not attending to my breasts. Before the month's end, I called the imaging center and scheduled the appointment for another 30 days out. During this self-imposed waiting period I didn't touch my breasts or even pay them a passing glance as I walked around my apartment half dressed. *Maybe if I'm very quiet and ignore them, they'll go away*, I thought.

The morning of my appointment, the receptionist asked me if I was currently feeling anything as she gestured to my chest without saying the word. *Just fear and existential angst*, I thought. "No, this is just a routine procedure my doctor wanted," I said with a keen awareness of the other women in the waiting room. It seemed overly personal to ask such a question at a front desk.

"So, no leaking, bumps, or discharge at all?" she asked in monotone, staring at her screen and typing.

"Nope," I said as my palms grew clammy. I assumed I wouldn't feel anything if something actually was amiss, which set a new fear aflame in my chest.

After 15 minutes of flipping through magazines without reading a word, a nurse called my name. She sent me down the hall to disrobe. As I changed into the half gown, I stared at my breasts in the bathroom mirror. It was the first time I'd looked at them in months. Reaching my arms over my head I realized they sat lower than when I was a tween examining myself against cartoon pictures. Maybe they weren't so bad, I decided, despite the space in between and slightly uneven size.

In the thin half robe, I sat and waited in another room faux-flipping through more magazines and thinking about my mom who likely sat and waited in a room similar to this one. I thought about how scared she must have felt even though she never told me. Inside the examination room, the tech squirted warm gel on my breasts and moved the sonogram wand around, staring at the screen taking pictures in the exact way I watched countless techs do for my wife when our baby was cooking inside of her. All the sonogram techs are looking for signs of a new life and I hoped she wouldn't find any inside of me. "Everything looks good, but make sure you keep up with these early detection measures," she said, as if she could sense I didn't want any part of the process.

I left with a sunny sense of gratitude for my health, but emotionally drained. Walking out I thought again about *The Keeping and Care of You*. Nowhere did the book mention you had to be obsessed with your body's appearance or its individual pieces. The book's sole purpose was to equip 8-14 year old girls with factual knowledge about their changing bodies and practical steps for how to take care of themselves. Although technically fully developed and a decade past my first period, my body continued to contain the same sense of mystery and curiosity that it carried as a kid. I wished for more *Keeping and Care of You* editions. Presently, I coveted the fictional, *The Keeping and Care of You: Firmly Planted in Womanhood Edition*, but I knew eventually I'd need others: *Surprise, It's Perimenopause* and *Finally, Full Blown Menopause*.

Guideless, I was forced to surmise what good advice the American Girl Team would have for me. Maybe the opposite of dislike and discomfort didn't have to be sabotage. Likely I would never ascribe to unconditional self-acceptance, but maybe attempting to care for my body, even one I didn't always like or love, was radical in and of itself.

# Our Big Gay Jewish Christmas Tree

"At this point, Christmas trees are an American tradition, like apple pies and shopping on Black Friday," I said, my face flushing, to our rabbi, while my soon-to-be wife stepped on my foot underneath the diner booth.

"Well, I think it's confusing, having a Christmas tree and being a Jewish family," Rabbi Esther said.

This was back in 2016; it was our third premarital counseling session with the rabbi. The three of us were squeezed into a corner booth at the Tick Tock Diner in Manhattan, a retro restaurant across the street from Penn Station that's popular with commuters from New Jersey and Long Island. The restaurant rests against The New Yorker hotel, which was once known for being infested with bed bugs, or at least that's what a trendy girl from Hell's Kitchen once told me. Now, catching a glimpse of The New Yorker signage from three avenues away makes my skin itch.

Alissa and I knew Rabbi Esther would be a good fit for us during our initial interview; she was accomplished, robustly feminist, and vocal about the importance of marrying same-sex couples. Her unruly, hazel curls and sharp blazer stacked with shoulder pads evoked the word *broad*: a word I would use to categorize all of my favorite women. Up until this moment, the worst thing about the counseling sessions was the lighting in the diner, which caused my rosacea to flare up and spread across my cheeks. If the 1,000-watt fluorescent bulbs weren't enough to burn my face, Tick Tock Diner has an extra sprinkling of neon bulbs and multicolored chandeliers which made the room brighter and hotter than my skin could tolerate.

"Do you want to order something?" the rabbi asked, pausing the Christmas tree debate. I knew Alissa wanted a Diet Coke, but we never ordered anything because we weren't sure who was responsible for paying, and neither of us carried cash. Rabbi Esther flipped the page of her oversized legal pad and scribbled the date across the top, while reminding us for the third time that in the summer of 2017 she would be taking a group of newlyweds to Israel, and she wanted us to join the trip.

"I don't think it's confusing at all," I said, unable to change the subject. I watched my fingers tear apart a paper straw wrapper.

"My brother and I grew up in a home with Christmas trees, three separate nativity scenes, and we received advent calendars as Hanukkah gifts," I added, "and not for one second did any of it confuse my understanding of Judaism." Looking at my pile of rage trash, I tried reminding myself I was conversing with a rabbi not an internet troll. But I couldn't stop talking.

"My mom grew up Southern Baptist and decided that raising my brother and me in my father's religion, not hers, would serve us best. She sacrificed her entire family history of religion by giving us this gift of Judaism, so it seems like the least we can do to honor her is by having a tree. Christmas trees have nothing to do with the birth of Jesus. Having a tree is a way to hold onto the holiday feeling I felt as a kid," I said in one breath.

"Our children will absolutely not believe in Santa," Alissa chimed in, cutting off my diatribe and verbally body checking me.

Rabbi Esther's head held perfectly still as she watched us bicker. Her eyes moved left to right like a retro owl cuckoo clock. Occasionally she nodded, but I couldn't tell in agreement with whom.

"Of course, no Santa," I said.

But I continued to railroad the conversation. "It's just a tree," I said. "We don't decorate it with angels or crucifixes, just colorful bulbs and nondenominational ornaments. Getting ready for Christmas was a meaningful activity at my house. I want my kids to have that feeling too."

With an authoritative raise of Rabbi Esther's hand I stopped speaking. If I were a cartoon, smoke stacks would have shot from my ears and nose.

"The holidays were a time of the year when everyone came together and continued traditions," Rabbi Esther said, completing my thought. "Coming together and continuing traditions is a great way to celebrate the holidays - but as a Jewish family you and Alissa should form Jewish rituals."

Hearing Rabbi Esther easily wrap her head around the idea of two women marrying and procreating while struggling to understand two Jews having a Christmas tree struck me as odd, but I kept those thoughts silent. Looking down at the table, I noticed my pile of rage trash had grown half an inch as I crumbled up more paper from a second straw wrapper. Our hour was nearly up.

"This is something you can keep discussing as a couple, and your thoughts will likely evolve," Rabbi Esther said, ending our session. I sipped my ice water and stared at my mountain of paper balls.

That year, our apartment lacked any holiday cheer. I conceded to the idea that Jews shouldn't have trees, and therefore dumped all of our holiday adornments down the trash chute. I worried that maybe allowing such items in our home was a watering down of Judaism, and therefore dangerous to maintaining our heritage.

However, two years after the Tick Tock Diner tree debacle, Alissa and I welcomed a baby boy into our family. And nine months later, when the holiday season arrived, Alissa and I both felt compelled to decorate. This tug to spruce up our apartment reminded me of the nesting prior to our son's birth; we wanted his eyes to be filled with lights and sparkle and magic. We decided it would be kosher to trim the apartment with blue and silver garland intermixed with white lights. A blue and white family of snowmen greeted us in our entryway, and Alissa agreed to let me hang my mother's multicolored bubble lights, as they carried a sentimental history. Still, no tree stood in our home.

I spent the season looking at the corner of our apartment where a petite, all-American artificial tree would fit. I said nothing, though, content enough watching the bubble lights recycle themselves around and around the glass candles on our windowsill.

Then, in March, just two weeks before our son's first birthday, the coronavirus arrived in the U.S. Our son had spent his first 14 days on earth in the NICU, so we had been looking forward to a blowout party for family and friends to celebrate. A week before the party, we sent out a mass cancellation text - becoming among the first wave of disappointed pandemic parents. Our son devoured his first bites of cake, vanilla with chocolate frosting, surrounded by his grandparents, an aunt, and Sesame Street posters. For the following five weeks, we kept the posters hanging above his highchair as Elmo's cartoon smile made our son laugh every time he entered the kitchen; it felt like the least we could do.

Like all pandemic parents, we've been innovating as we go. Months later, the morning after a socially distanced Halloween in which our son didn't wear a costume, the thought of holiday directions entered my mind. I was reaching for a way to brighten up the dark times creeping back into the city. Before I could even speak up, Alissa looked at me over our first cup of coffee one morning and said, "We should get a tree this year, right?"

"If ever there was a year to get a tree, I'd say a global pandemic is it," I responded.

We settled on the compact three foot tall, white, prelit, plastic variety. In pursuit of maintaining our Judaism, all the ornaments that year were blue and silver with a scattering of New York City themed pieces; a black and white cookie, pickle, empire state building, and menorah topper. Our kid spent the weeks pulling off the bulbs and rolling them all around the living room like bowling balls. Each night as the sun set, he reminded us to turn on the tree lights. As COVID surged we made the decision to not visit with any of our extended family, a first for us all. In the dark holiday season where COVID was peaking and the vaccine was still a fantasy, I appreciated the tree's light and the sense of spirit it brought to our space.

Coronavirus aside, I suspect we would have naturally arrived at a place of "yes" in regard to the tree. As a parent, you want to give your children joy and traditions during the holidays. And even though I grew up having a bat mitzvah and love for lox, Christmas trees were a part of my family's holiday fabric, and I don't want to let that go. Given the increasing variance in the ways people live their lives, giving up a Christmas tree for the sake of religion seemed archaic.

Rabbi Esther was right, of course. Our conversation has evolved. I'm a gay Jewish American with a Christian parent, and having a seasonal tree is a part of my family's new world identity. A tree doesn't make us any less Jewish or more American; it isn't complicated, the same way having two moms isn't. Our gay Jewish holiday tree is the embodiment of what the melting pot values of America should be: sparkling, allied, and, above all, hopeful.

## Southern Charm

"Who let those dykes in here?" a sorority sister asked, pointing at me and Alissa from across the dining room. Earlier that day, we had become the unwitting targets of a "dyke" rumor that spread like wildfire to the entire sorority. As we shoveled baked spaghetti onto our plates in shame, another sister assured us she didn't believe it. The irony of that moment is that Alissa and I weren't even dating yet. We hadn't had our first kiss or held hands, but the chemistry between us was palpable enough that our sisters could sense it. Guess I wasn't hiding my feelings well enough.

*I can do better*, I thought, berating myself and making a mental list of guys to publicly kiss the following weekend.

In another lifetime, maybe our sorority sisters would have teased us to "get together already." But in our Southern sorority in the late aughts, it was unacceptable. Despite being submerged in the pain and humiliation from the original rumor and subsequent ones to follow, Alissa and I fell in love.

For the past decade, I've recounted our origin story with levity. I tell people we initially found having a secret relationship thrilling. Some of that is true, but in reality, we were hiding. Feeling like you need to conceal who you are-and the person you are falling in love with-is scary and dehumanizing. It's also heartbreaking to fall in love for the first time with no one to witness it.

By the time I rushed in the fall of 2007, my sophomore year, I knew I preferred kissing girls, but I had convinced myself I could tuck that truth away until graduation. Radford

University, my undergraduate alma mater in Virginia, is a small state school nestled in the New River Valley near the Blue Ridge Mountains, less than 200 miles from the West Virginia border. The town was predominantly white and conservative, both in religion and politics. While the campus contained pockets of left-leaning organizations, it wasn't a place known for its highly visible or diverse queer scene.

At an off-campus party during my first week of freshman year, I overheard a boy casually, and extremely comfortably, call someone a "kike." I had grown accustomed to being one of just a few Jewish students at my high school outside of Richmond, but I had never encountered emboldened hatred toward Jewish people. While the culture shock in college made me uncomfortable, I didn't let it show. I learned to shut up, smile, and keep my otherness to myself. At 19, I more or less looked the part of a typical Southern college girl. And aside from hiding my sexuality, I was generally enjoying being on my own for the first time.

When I was initiated, I promised myself that I'd stop kissing girls when I got drunk. I promised myself that I'd focus on fitting in and having cool frat guys think I was hot. At the time, I hadn't examined *why* I thought I wanted that attention; I hadn't learned about compulsive heterosexuality, which can cause people, especially women, to assume they are interested in male attention.

For a few weeks I made friends with the older sisters, snorted cheap cocaine, binge drank, and took on hazing like it was my sport. I fucked frat guys without catching feelings, as only dykes can, and was rewarded with emotional high fives from my sisters along the way. For a moment, I was the embodiment of the "cool girl" monologue from *Gone Girl*. The fake version of myself felt like she belonged.

But the rules I thought I understood quickly turned against me. When Alissa and I started hooking up, I kept seeing random guys to save face. She accepted it, which allowed us to pretend our feelings weren't as serious as they were. Looking back, I hate that I felt the need to push against my natural feelings of attraction.

During my spring semester, I hooked up with a boy from a popular fraternity. I assumed it would earn me social credit. In a not-so-shocking turn of events, he announced our hookup at his next chapter meeting, which was met by roars of approval. Not one older sorority sister comforted me or even asked about it. I was humiliated, but I welcomed the reprieve of being called a slut instead of a dyke.

Shortly after that, I stopped forcing myself to feign interest in guys. It became harder to fake it after Alissa and I started saying *I love you*. The two of us began spending most of our free time together, locked away in her bedroom making out as girls fluttered throughout the sorority house around us.

One night, Alissa and I crashed a random house party with a group of our friends. The seductive boom of '90s R&B, and memories of middle school dances lured us inside. Unlike the sweaty, grinding basement parties we were used to, everyone here danced in an almost juvenile way. The energy reminded me of being 13 years old at a Bar Mitzvah afterparty. Our friends disappeared inside, getting drinks and flirting with the onslaught of new guys. Alissa and I found our way into the middle of the room and started dancing together.

Nothing about us that night would have raised an eyebrow, but to me it felt electric. We stayed on the dance floor for over an hour. Alissa twirled around me and rapped every word to Notorious BIG's "Juicy," while I laughed, astonished at the juxtaposition between her jean skirt preppy style and ability to seamlessly rap. Whitney Houston's "I Wanna Dance with Somebody" played, and she grabbed my hands, twisting me back and forth. This moment was what I wanted my life to feel like. A desperate part of me hoped someone might notice we were in love.

After graduation, Alissa and I separately battled our own coming-out journeys. It took another three years for our relationship to be fully public. Alissa's best friend from the sorority came to visit us a few months after we confided in her. We knew it might initially be awkward, but we weren't expecting her to say that she didn't accept it or announce, while we were all drunk at a club, that she would pray for us.

Queer people are master survivors, and a large part of that survival is storytelling, specifically how we craft our own narratives. It has been easier for me to spin our origin story, to myself and others, as a lighthearted, even funny tale. But the truth is that falling in love secretly is daunting. The good thing about stories is that they are ongoing, and luckily there are now parts of ours that are wholly joyful.

On a chilly November morning, two years after we moved to New York City, Alissa and I decided to get married. I can't recall the words exchanged or who proposed the idea. The moment lives as a sense memory: soft legs intertwined underneath cool cotton sheets, my eyes heavy, having only been open for mere minutes, the heat of our 15-pound poodle still asleep underneath the comforter, the crisp light of late fall pouring in through our window, creating a bright rectangle across the bed and floor, my pulse calm and sure.

Marriage equality hadn't passed at the federal level, but it was legal in New York. Before moving to the city, we floated the idea of skipping a formal marriage, but looking back, maybe that was a product of our internalized homophobia. The realization that we could have a wedding with our friends and family became easier to visualize once we were surrounded by so many queer people.

Since living in the city, the idea of marriage had been a casual conversation over diner pancakes and on rambling city walks, but in this moment, it transformed into a concrete plan. Underneath sheets warmed by our bodies we laughed and mused about what our parents would say. From the office of our bed, we made the calls; everyone screamed and cheered. We laid daydreaming out loud for hours.

While I'd never planned a wedding, I did assist in the planning of my Bat Mitzvah, which was strikingly similar in checklists and stress level. The anxiety leading up to my Bat Mitzvah exceeded typical teen nerves. My Sunday school classmates shouted about DJs, party themes, and who they hoped to dance with during the slow songs. My best friend Emma walked me through an elaborate balloon sculpture designed as a 6-foot version of her in a hula skirt complete with coconut bra. Said balloon sculpture would reside in her bedroom for three years past the event.

None of the exciting party aspects overrode my stress.

Aside from the mortifying act of chanting, I also had to read pages of Hebrew. While the majority of my classmates had spent the last seven years at Wednesday school learning Hebrew, I had been practicing pirouettes. At 13 being seen on a good day was uncomfortable, so the thought of being seen on a bema in front of my congregation, half of my middle school, and family while reading Hebrew was unbearable.

I survived leading the service without stroking out. Most of the afterparty is a blacked-out blur. However unbearable, it's what we do as Jews and I am glad my parents made me continue the tradition. The ceremony, while excruciating for me, is now a part of my family's storytelling. My grandmother, the showgirl of our family, "forgot" her reading glasses and made a spectacle, borrowing the rabbi's to read off a prayer card (of a prayer she had likely memorized by age 4). My granny, the most supportive Southern Baptist, took a photo with me with the widest, proudest smile she ever made. It's a photo I cherish from a woman who notoriously looked miserable in pictures. The night before my Friday night service my favorite aunt gifted me a Tiffany necklace, which was the first nice piece of jewelry I owned and wore for a decade. On the ride over to the reception we crammed into my family's minivan chock-full of balloons. My dad couldn't see out any of the windows and no one could help him as we were all enveloped by pink latex. My mom bought me purple sparkle gel pens to write thank you notes and helped me address envelopes while we watched our Thursday night lineup a week later.

I never had the knowing sense that I'd grow up and get

married despite this being a more common rite of passage. When I met Alissa and our relationship developed, we both felt similarly about being too seen in such a formal manner. She had experienced a similar mortification via Bat Mitzvah. Both of us felt like weddings were often tacky and overly expensive. The idea of City Hall and taking our family out to lunch sounded romantic and more in line with our personalities.

Alissa and I decided on a two-year engagement. We'd already been together for six years and we didn't feel like a rush. The idea of a small ceremony occurred often in our discussions. Maybe we'd get married in Central Park and then take everyone out to eat at a diner. Maybe we would go to City Hall and then go out to a bar. Maybe just the two of us and our immediate families would be present. We tested out the idea of not having a full ceremony and party and people responded in horror. My childhood friend Emma burst into tears over a vodka soda at a bar when we floated the idea to her. She couldn't fathom not bearing witness to our marriage.

"Please you have to do something, even if it's small," she pleaded. It was hard to find reasons not to have a celebration, so we started planning an intimate but festive occasion complete with typical wedding paraphernalia; rabbis, flowers, café lights, and save the dates.

A year and one month out from our wedding date, we were still mulling over wedding plans. On an average summer day, we boarded the Hampton Jitney to visit Alissa's family in Southampton for the weekend. I looked forward to swimming in her grandmother's 85-degree pool and watching our dog run on the beach. An hour into the bus ride my phone started buzzing. Alissa's phone buzzed. Chatter erupted. With the striking of a mallet, marriage equality had passed and gay people all across the United States now had equal federal rights to marry.

I found myself stewing about missing family stories and gaps in ancestral trees. It struck me that generations of gay couples didn't have photo albums with pictures of fathers toasting and sisters dancing. These couples never had frozen cakes in their freezers or even a 4x7 on a nightstand showing the night they looked gorgeous and started off a life together with support of friends and family. A quiet and invisible life was the best many couples could manage.

I obsessed about missing familial folklore: cousins getting too drunk at afterparties and best friends catching garter belts. We're void of generations of gay love stories ending in weddings. It was a hole in our country's history I was determined to fill with flowers, good wine, party music, and dancing.

It feels otherworldly that three weeks before Alissa and I exchanged vows I was assaulted. The compartments of my brain worked overtime to separate that day from the rest of my life. My body helped too as it healed superficially. By the time our big day arrived not a bruise or scratch remained from his hands or the struggle of the night. Somehow, no preoccupations or recurring thoughts bothered my mind for the days before and after our wedding. We were busy with last minute wedding prep, but I was also excited. I had gone from a girl who never daydreamed of weddings or marriages to a woman who couldn't wait to say, "I do."

We broke most archaic traditions and conducted the day the way we wanted to. Rule breaking is easier when you're already living outside the expected social contract. We spent the night before the wedding together and the morning alone. We ventured to Hollywood Diner in Chelsea before meeting everyone at the hair salon. Over bagels and fried eggs, we whispered about the enormity of the day ahead and giggled knowing that no one else in the restaurant knew.

Our wedding day is now imprinted, quilted into our family's histories. We have expanded the narrative for everyone. Everyone who attended now carries stories about their morning, hotel stays, and what they wore. During cocktail hour guests joked about how the rabbi pronounced *huppah*, which has turned into an ongoing family joke. Our DJ, who was supposed to play us into the ceremony, was late, taking a phone call and smoking a cigarette right outside the venue while we stood inside. Alissa cried during the entire ceremony. In every photo from our vow exchange, she is wiping her eyes or has tears pictured on her cheeks. During the party, Alissa and I were one of the last couples on the dance floor, and this time I knew everyone could really see us.

# Part III:
# Motherland

# Shopping for Sperm

I had a hunch scrolling through human men to purchase wouldn't be as carefree as perusing the J. Crew website for new fall boots. Upon first glance two things were clear 1) human men were far more expensive than boots and 2) there was no return policy or lifetime guarantee on these guys. I didn't even want to shop for sperm in the first place. Ideally, I wanted to conceive a baby from both my wife's and my DNA, a baby who would be an amalgamation of our best and worst parts. At this point in history, my longing was merely a medical pipe dream. So here we were, shopping for sperm online.

Before the process officially started, Alissa assured me selecting sperm would be fine.

"It's what we have to do in order to get the end result we want. Lots of people have to go through this process," she said. "There isn't one way to make a family," she continued in her optimistic pump-up speech. Alissa insisted I was overthinking the situation and was frustrated with my uncertainty about the life-alerting endeavor we were starting. Attempting to soothe my nerves, she promised me the baby would love watching Bravo TV and would appreciate the nuances between various black and white cookies, as these are valuable life skills you can teach a child and are not genetically coded.

The process of picking out sperm was shockingly akin to online dating. You paid a company a specified amount of money per month in order to view profiles and click buttons that could effectively change the trajectory of your life. Our fertility center sent us a short list of cryobanks and highlighted their endorsement based on ethical standards and reported patient satisfaction. Trusting the experts, we logged onto the website and were greeted by a homepage emblazoned with pictures of smiling children conceived through successful IUI and IVF. Their bright faces reassured me, and a sudden yearning pulsed through my chest. Alissa anxiously typed in our credit card information and with a flash of the screen we were granted access to the donor section. The page is filled with seemingly endless rows of baby pictures belonging to donors of every race, ethnicity, and skin tone imaginable. After a mere 60 seconds of clicking boxes, it was painfully apparent picking out sperm was overwhelming, and not, in fact, fine.

"I told you this was weird," I said deflated. For once, being right provided no ego boost or endorphin rush. Alissa felt heavyhearted about rummaging through the never-ending pages of strange men. The breadth of information you could ascertain about each donor was staggering, and it could be even more dizzying for an additional $100.00, which we didn't pay because frankly hearing a sound clip of the donor's voice or reading his haiku defining his spirituality would have sent us into a mental paralysis.

After hardly five minutes of searching, Alissa shut the computer screen with a firm hand. "I'm sorry," I said, wishing I could make it easier. I watched my wife's enthusiasm dissolve into a puddle of heartbreak. It was the first time the weight of our situation hit her.

"I want *our* baby," Alissa said, snuggled into my neck

later that night in bed. "This feels like a science experiment and I don't want *any* sperm." I giggled at the obviousness of two lesbians renouncing sperm altogether. It was a maddening feeling, out of control over the process of how our life was unfolding. Alissa is especially keen on maneuvering through life with her personal precision and found the act of surrendering almost unmanageable.

Early on in our lives, queer people are faced with the realization that if they choose to live an out life, then the way we move through the world, how we are perceived, and what parts of mainstream life we have access to will not be of the norm. In many ways, this gives us a built-in freedom to thoughtfully design our lives based on desire and wants, not cultural expectations. Mostly, I revel in this expansiveness. While the end has always been right, the moment of not being able to combine DNA with the person I loved most to create a child of our own felt unfair and tragic. Half a decade removed from this moment, I can see the truth. We did create a baby on our own. The son we have would not exist in the world if we hadn't dreamt him up. He quite literally would not be on this planet without the two of us. My initial reflex to have this perceived "inability" to conceive was rooted in believing the heteronormative was the right way or best way. It is a long and ever continuing road to deconstruction.

Six days later, after we finished sitting an emotional shiva, we hunkered down and began a serious comb through of choices. We started checking relevant filters based on what felt essential for our family. Aside from overall health, Alissa declared ensuring profiles possessed adult photographs was the most crucial filter to check. She refused to even glance at a profile not containing an adult photo. While most children can be perceived as cute this is obviously not the case for adults, and it was a risk she wouldn't take. She found it wildly suspicious if a donor hadn't submitted at least three recent photos of himself.

According to everyone, Alissa and I have similar physical qualities, so choosing a male donor resembling me turned out to be a male resembling her. Ten years of being stopped and asked, "Are you guys sisters?" was finally paying off. It has continuously struck me odd the sheer volume of people who choose to ask us this question. Whether we sit soaking with our feet in pedicure tubs or sucking down lattes at a cafe, grown adults have routinely felt more than comfortable asking us if we're related. Most recently, we were walking our dog in search of gelato when a man in a moving truck stopped his attempt at parallel parking to stick his head out the driver side window and loudly announce, "You girls look like sisters!" in a thick Jersey accent. Adults seem to have a deep compulsion to label everyone. Generally, we don't respond to these statements, but on occasion one of us will chime in "No, this is my wife" out of a need to be seen for who we are. We used to throw in, "Just sorority sisters!" but that's too long and old of a story at this point.

We began sifting through our narrowed choices of men who all possessed goofy sentence long names like, "blue eyes on the beach," "surfs up, smiles out," and my favorite, "clowning around with purpose." Only five men remained. It was essentially the fastest episode of the *Bachelorette* where no one received a rose. It didn't feel good to be choosing a donor for our future child like a Tinder date. We both simply wanted a kind, smart, attractive donor. Neither one of us was interested in creating a designer baby in spite of the myriad of options making it seem like we should.

By this point in our search the crop of men we sorted through were similar; brown hair, brown eyes, Jew(ish), seemed to love their mothers, and didn't appear to be complete psychopaths, although this was difficult to gauge. I guess we'll have to wait 20 years to see if we correctly sorted that piece out. For a moment, we became hung up on the medical family histories realizing some of our favored contenders had blemishes on their records. We realized, however, if we were able to physically conceive a child, we would bring together a storm of serious medical and mental health issues, so suddenly these blips didn't seem so alarming.

I found myself exceedingly preoccupied with the "about me" section filled out by donors. One prospective candidate seemed like a possibility, but then wrote that the most adventurous moment he experienced was hunting for black bears, which was a hard pass for me. Upon further inspection, he answered "who would you have lunch with dead or alive" by stating: "his current girlfriend." Zero points for imagination. Next.

We inspected a wannabe filmmaker whose favorite childhood memory was of his mother and him reading *Harry Potter* which was heartwarming, but then he listed his ideal lunch date as Bill Maher stating he "loves politics and thinks he's a cool guy." Next.

A close contender was a chunky baby with a toothless

grin who morphed into a sexy ripped surfer with dazzling eyes. After seeing his pictures, Alissa grew momentarily obsessed with the idea of our child growing up to be athletic, despite sports and athleticism never being a core value in our family. Under proudest accomplishment he listed: "recent improvements in boxing." Snooze. Also, he looked like a Hitler youth from certain angles. Next.

When we found *him*, we knew.

We both attempted to play it cool, mentioned we should keep searching, but it was obvious. We knew the same way it was clear in college we belonged to one another, in spite of us spending a few years trying to escape it. *He* felt unavoidable and cosmic. His personal essay melted my insides with its sincerity and gentleness. While we decided to keep details about the donor private, I will divulge he wanted to have lunch unironically with Mr. Rogers and staring at his childhood photos made an egg drop from my ovary.

I texted Alissa at work the next day and told her I'd spent the morning staring at baby pictures of *him* and fantasizing about what our own baby's smile would look like. She sent back a flutter of hearts to my phone.

Suddenly, nothing about this conception felt artificial or overly scientific. It felt a lot like love, which I think is what making a baby is supposed to be anyway.

# Belly Envy

"I wish we had a husband," I said to my wife. She was 32 weeks pregnant, and I was carrying the lion's share of our groceries back to our apartment, three blocks over and one street up. I had surprised myself when I first said this phrase a few weeks earlier, practically spitting it out. Now, I said it almost daily.

Before my wife got pregnant, the division of labor in our home was a utopian 50/50, sorted out by skill set and preference. If anything, my haphazard regard for household minutiae, paired with my wife's attention to detail, had let me off the hook for many annoying tasks. But as my wife's pregnancy progressed, my participation in manual chores increased. In the span of one week, I stood atop a step ladder to rearrange a high cabinet, employed a screwdriver on three separate occasions, and reconnected our Apple TV. These tasks, coupled with my fetus-free body, accumulated into a sense of masculinity I had never wanted and grew to resent.

In the beginning, the process of creating our family was collaborative. Both of us assumed we would carry a child at some point, so we decided that my wife, being one year older, would go first. Together, we thoughtfully chose a donor and fertility specialist and coincided our calendars to allow us both to attend the full gamut of appointments, from monitoring every 3 days to the end game of insemination. After an IUI treatment, we impatiently waited 14 days and then scrutinized the pregnancy test stick. We celebrated when the test showed two lines and began brainstorming baby names and visualizing how to best rearrange our one-bedroom Brooklyn apartment to accommodate our upcoming addition.

As the summer heat dissipated and hot coffee replaced iced, my wife's belly expanded in correlation with my own unexpected feelings of anxiety. At doctors' appointments, receptionists, nurses, and doctors asked my wife, "Who have you brought along for the visit?" Nobody batted an eye once proper introductions were exchanged, but their first impression stayed with me. I was viewed, initially, as a tagalong in this process, not an equal partner.

At home I felt helpless. My compulsion to share in caring for our budding fetus transformed me into a nudge. Without consulting any experts, I created a list of house rules for her including: do not stand on the step ladder, use extra caution when entering and exiting the shower, do not carry items weighing more than 15 pounds. In the afternoons, I found myself interrogating my wife about the nutritional value of her packed lunch, to ensure she was eating enough for herself and our sea monkey-sized life. At night, I asked if she had taken her numerous, horse pill-sized prenatal vitamins, even though she never missed a day. At all hours, I pushed glasses of water in her direction, noting that I had once read that pregnant women needed three times the amount of water as the rest of us. I knew I was being overbearing, but I couldn't stop because, in a way, the nagging felt like caretaking.

About four months into the pregnancy, my wife began feeling him move. These movements couldn't be felt from the outside yet, and I started to develop a complex. Like a lesbian-specific version of Freud's penis envy, I was seething with pregnancy belly envy. Nobody had warned me that not physically carrying the baby could cause a sudden onset of jealousy. Even when my wife audibly winced from a fetal foot pressing into her rib cage, I coveted her pain, craving the touch of his tiny limbs. My jealousy sprung up when I imagined his half-developed fetus ears listening to her favorite music on the way to work and hearing her office friends throughout the day. More than once, I caught myself imagining unzipping him off her body to take him out for coffee with my friends, hearing the sounds and voices of my everyday life.

About a month later, I could feel the baby move from the outside, which brought about a small sense of relief-and new fixation with getting him to move for me. Coming home from work I would loudly announce myself at above indoor voice-levels and make a racket putting my things away. "The baby always kicks when you start talking," my wife said. It might have been a coincidence-or a lie of generosity-but I appreciated the notion. I found ways to gently push on her stomach and certain songs to sing that could get him to stir. My connection to him began feeling more tangible and I loosened up on my pestering, except for the step ladder ban and water intake.

I assumed my belly envy had run its course until one night, mere weeks before our due date. We were getting ready for bed, chatting about our soon-to-be son, and suddenly I was sobbing. For the first time, it occurred to me that this tiny human, who I already loved so much, would share DNA with my wife's parents, sister, cousins, aunts, and uncles. Intellectually, I knew I would be this boy's mother.

I knew all families were created differently. And I knew from personal experience that genes in and of themselves don't guarantee closeness and love. But in that moment, it felt heartbreakingly unfair that her entire lineage would share something with him that I never could, and it left me wondering, again, about my contribution.

Through heaves, I told my wife I worried the baby wouldn't be connected to me. She acknowledged my frustration and assured me that by taking good care of her over the past 10 months I had also been taking good care of the baby. I had lugged heavy bags full of food that eventually got to his tiny belly, screwed the bolts to his dresser, and assembled his bassinet. I nodded in agreement, letting the words register and feeling somewhat reassured. My previously unwanted masculine role translated, on some level, into that of a solid care provider.

An exhausted pregnant woman, my wife fell asleep moments after the conversation, leaving me to mull my feelings over alone. I recognized her speech was nice and true, but I felt even better when I remembered something she had pointed out weeks earlier. There was one thing I could do-and she couldn't-to get in some early bonding time. I leaned over and whispered into her belly, an action physically out of range for her. I began to chatter-directly in his almost fully formed ears-about my day, what was happening on the latest episode of *Real Housewives*, and all the fun things his mom and I had planned for him when he was ready to arrive. This didn't fully resolve the envy and disconnection anxiety, but sparked the obvious fact, soon he would be on the other side, and these fears wouldn't hold.

# Anxiety of Being the Non-bio Parent

It was decided in a practical manner that my wife would carry our first child, as she was older and seemed keener on the idea. She quickly conceived through IUI, and as the months progressed, I began worrying about where I fit into this baby's life, as he wasn't biologically mine and I wasn't carrying him. I developed belly envy - a lesbian-specific Freudian self-diagnosis similar to penis envy - yearning for a physical body that could never be mine. Watching my wife partake in what appeared to be the beginning stages of caretaking and bonding left me feeling useless. I wanted to experience the mystical sensation of my son moving inside my body. My wife and I managed and struggled through my feelings, and just when I felt like I was coming to terms with the pregnancy, he arrived.

With a swift cut of the umbilical cord, I was a mother. *We* were mothers. I knew I loved him right away, but I wasn't sure how he felt about me. I worried he couldn't recognize my smell like he could with his other mom, the one whom he had lived inside. My wife was inundated with the things you say about a brand-new baby: "He looks just like you, he looks just like your dad, I see so much of your great-grandpa in him." Examining this squishy-faced, steely-eyed baby with a mop of curly hair, I wasn't always sure these statements were true, and they grated on my nerves, alternately enraging me on days when I caught a glimpse of him and recognized the truth in what others said. He, my wife, and my father-in-law all have unmistakable matching cleft chins. His hair does look like my wife's hair did when she was an infant. And it is possible his head shape matches that of his grandfather.

All of the external noise mixed with stress of keeping alive a newborn let loose a feral side of myself I never knew existed - an urge to swallow him whole and keep him inside of myself, just so he would know he too belonged to me, an impulse to take him and my wife far away. It worried me that he might catch a whiff of my wife's family and the aromatic DNA signals would tell him that he belonged to them, leaving me out. Seeing other people hold him would send a primal compulsion through me to rip him out of their arms. Immediately after this thought, a deep sadness settled into my chest. I love my extended family. Since Day 1, they have loved me like their own. Marriage and baby aside, my extended family is my family. It was confusing, the urge to create distance from them, but when we were all together, I felt left out, the one without matching blood. I hated that he had cousins, great uncles, and aunts that shared something with him that I never would. At times, it felt like a gaping hole of grief I'd never be able to fill.

When it was just the three of us, I felt more at ease. I felt deeply connected to him, but the back of my brain itched with worries about him feeling more attached to my wife, as she had carried him for the past 10 months and brought him into the world. It's difficult to tell with newborns as they scream, make sweet sounds, and take bottles from anyone who'll offer. You are always waiting for a definitive sign. I was in the fog of early parenthood one day or night, sitting on the couch holding his wailing body and trying to ready his bottle, when he settled and sucked away calmly looking at me with doe eyes, as if he hadn't just been howling in my face for 10 straight minutes. Outside of our 10th floor apartment window, the sky lit up with lightning in bright, mile-wide streaks. It was silent and there was no rain. Another morning, I sat with him completing a similar routine when three red balloons floated across the morning sky. At the time it all felt important. I liked knowing we shared these moments and realizing we were creating something of our very own.

As an infant, my son was fickle and a screamer, especially between the hours of 6 to 9 PM Our world would appear fine and then *the* scream would escape his small lungs, filling the apartment for 45 minutes at a time. I was best at calming him during these upheavals. Using the self-patented combination of holding him tightly against my chest as I walked across the apartment doing leg lunges and then circled him in a *Lion King*-like motion, he would eventually calm or at least scream at a lower octave. Everyone noticed I was good with him when he became otherwise inconsolable, and it felt satisfying. He must know me, I thought, despite not having matching DNA or an identical chin cleft.

Soon after, my thoughts began shifting away from his relationship to others. As all new parents quickly understand, you are the expert. Within weeks, I could change his diaper in the middle of the night, in a pitch black room with ease, I knew the angle to feed and burp him, and only Alissa and I knew the correct number of "Shh's" mixed with bouncing to make him fall asleep in our arms when he was ready to nap. Visitors quickly handed him over to one of us when he fussed or spit up or blew out a diaper. Over time, my thoughts and worries lost their weight as they did not match up with reality. He was bonding most obviously to both of us.

Another magical phenomenon occurred; I found myself springing awake from a deep sleep and 30 seconds later, as if I had conjured him up myself, the baby would begin to cry, ready to eat. It felt reassuring to know him and be connected to him on a subconscious level. During these moments I began to understand what current science was reporting, that the brain scans of parents mapped themselves to their child as they bonded, whether or not they were biologically related. As the months passed, the baby's attachment became more obvious, and my mind rattled with fewer worried thoughts about him.

When my wife holds him, their physical similarities are illuminated and it now makes my insides swell, as I can't imagine him being luckier to look like anyone else. The fear of being left out dims day by day when he lights up to see me, reaches for me, and frankly has begun stalking me. Right before his first birthday, my son became overtly obsessed with us, screeching if we leave the room for one second, walking right into our laps, and doing anything his body is capable of to make us laugh or smile at him. This new obsessive love makes me more easily appreciate him having the matching face and frame of his grandfather. Thinking about his DNA being the same as his extended family now feels easier too. I know much of myself and my own family will be nurtured into him. He'll be balanced, not because of the molecules that run through him, but because he has deep relationships with people who love him.

My thoughts and body have changed since his arrival; my brain is more occupied, newly formed bags reside under my eyes, and I recently found my first gray hair. Every day it becomes more clear, bonding is not based in blood, but in every action and interaction my son and I exchange.

# It's Not the Dinosaur Shirt that Makes the Man

In 2018, after two rounds of IUI, my wife conceived, and we both assumed she was brewing a girl. "I can feel it, I know it," my wife said when discussing the sex of the baby. And I believed her; her sense of her body had never been wrong. I know gender is a construct and it doesn't matter what you refer to a fetus as, but the point is, I had a way in which I thought things would go. For weeks, we referred to the baby bump as she and her.

We waltzed into our 22-week ultrasound appointment and were dumbfounded when the technician waved a wand across my wife's stomach announcing, "Congratulations, it's a boy." I quickly recovered, knowing I'd be happy to have whomever we received, but a disappointed beat did bounce through me.

At the time, aside from a handful of men related to me by blood or marriage, my life was barren of men. As a young adult, I'd tried using men as a form of unsuccessful sexual corrective therapy, and a way to seem normal to my sorority sisters, but by the time I was 30, I had married a woman and my closest confidants were all females.

As a writer, I wrote for women, specifically queer women, and once I accepted that notion, I never wondered or worried about how my work or life affected men. Eventually, the whole cis male gender was an afterthought. "If they want to do the work, they can figure it out," I'd always say. Building a good man wasn't my job.

Until it was. After the ultrasound, I realized I had to start understanding men, boys, and their perception of the world. Suddenly, it felt like my responsibility to figure out how to build a more ethical male. Of course, I recognized that perhaps my son would actually be my daughter or a queer person, but I felt more suited for those truths. It was statistically likely I would be raising a cis straight man, a group of people who I felt a deep apathy for. Until then, their experience was not mine to consider or take on. I didn't care if they participated in the evolving world around me. Before we left the doctor's office I felt a softness and curiosity grow. I thought about my younger brother and the sweet and excitable personality he had as a little boy. Begrudgingly I knew men weren't the problem but the system in which we raised them.

My first step was to tackle his nursery. "No construction work theme, or dinosaurs, and please not too much blue," I said to my wife as we scrolled through artwork on Etsy. We settled on zoo animals, some of which were wearing tiny blue bow ties, but my wife placated me by declaring the giraffe to be a handsome butch woman. When it came to baby clothing, we avoided anything deemed too masculine - monster trucks, footballs, race cars - and we forbid any heteronormative sexualized apparel ("Ladies Man;" "Watch Out, Girls"). It would be all rainbow stripes, bear faces, and polka dots for our little one.

When our son arrived, I was astounded at my immediate attachment, swift and consuming. There is nothing gendered about babies, so for months I forgot all the ethical boy-building and was overwhelmed with his smooshiness, warmth, and the way his meatball hands and sausage fingers grasped my palm.

Gender wasn't top of mind most of his first year. He was simply our baby. The first months were a blur of diapers, bottles, cuddles, and sleep deprivation - there was little time to think about building a better man.

As more months passed and our lives leveled back out, his gender identity eventually sprung back into my consciousness. Statistically, I realized he'd likely be a straight male, at least until he notified us otherwise. And if he were a straight male, I realized, I'd already made obvious errors. While I wasn't allowing him to wear firetruck onesies, I had been referring to him as "the Prince of Park Slope" for the past 11 months. Furthermore, I was constantly telling him how beautiful, funny, and smart he was. Had I already initiated the first step in creating an entitled egomaniac? It dawned on me that keeping him away from certain T-shirts was not likely the answer to raising a better boy.

"We have to stop calling him The Prince of Park Slope," I said to my wife over dinner.

"I heard they call him The President of MyGym," she said, which was a local play center he attended five times a week.

"Well, he is a genius and the cutest, of course they call him that!" I said, not being able to help myself but now feeling sure I was creating an arrogant monster.

At 18 months, it became harder to enforce our gendered clothing rules as he began demonstrating his own preferences, which leaned heavily on vehicles. He loved construction trucks, city buses, garbage trucks, and anything flying in the sky; his poor index finger must have felt exhausted from all the pointing while we were outside.

His grandma, taking note of his budding interest, bought him a shirt covered in construction trucks. He loved to look down at it and point and squeak in excitement. For good measure, I gave him a baby doll, which he occasionally hugged and pretended to feed, but most days he preferred jamming rocks into his trucks and collecting sticks on walks. I let him enjoy it all, of course, knowing I'd be a hypocrite if I stood in the way of his natural curiosity.

After begrudgingly accepting his interests, while of course still forcing him to listen to showtunes and detailing the newest storyline of *Housewives*, I realized I didn't know then how to help him be a good man or not beyond simply avoiding gender stereotypes.

And then, at 20 months, he started to try to talk. The day was full of noises denoting a variety of feelings and thoughts. He screeched to let us know he didn't like the song playing on the TV or if he couldn't reach a toy. He howled, signaling that we were reading him the wrong book.

Listening to him try so hard to communicate had me thinking more about the ways in which social expectations can damage boys', then men's, ability to communicate. I thought of all the men I disdained - the misogynistic frat guy archetypes, the love you "no homo" bros, the gaslighters, the abusers, and "family values" politicians - and what they had in common.

*I'll teach him to talk about his feelings*, I decided. I'll teach him to ask for help, with confidence, as this seemed like a vital skill a subset of men were lacking! I'll teach him to proudly tell others when he's feeling sad or mad and even joyful. I'll let him know it's OK to cry. We'll talk about consent and respecting other people's words.

I may have been getting ahead of myself, but my toddler was there to bring me back to the present, screaming at the TV and looking at me to change the channel.

"Help me," I said, looking at him. "You say it: 'Help me.'" He paused, then parroted, "Hep mah" in a calmer, more relaxed voice. It wasn't perfect, but it was a good start. "Yay!" We both clapped at his attempt, and I changed the channel for him.

Another afternoon, he stood swatting at the kitchen table, trying to reach for his milk and grunting loudly. "Please," I said to him and waited. "Les" he said back before I handed him the cup.

"Thank you," I said, handing him half of a breakfast banana over our kitchen table. "Tank gu," he said, smiling back, knowing our new routine.

"If nothing else, he won't be rude," I said to my wife, who was at that moment prompting him to say, "Thank you," as she shared a spoonful of ice cream with him.

These short phrases and polite gestures won't fix everything, but it feels like the beginning of something. I know I can't mold him into the perfect feminist ally, or the perfect anything, but I have the suspicion that it isn't the dinosaur shirts or Tonka trucks that make the man.

I am starting to feel hopeful, too, that by letting him feel all his feelings and helping him learn how to ask for what he needs, he will turn out to be a decent human being, regardless of his gender.

# Medicinal Romance

Four years ago, my wife, Alissa, underwent infertility treatments to conceive our son. I was there for it all, standing by her side during the biweekly bloodwork, internal sonograms, and the IUI procedure. It's not that I was there for each moment of my wife's treatment because I'm an amazingly supportive spouse - of course, I'm also that, but I wanted to be there. I wanted to be a part of conception.

Conception: That magical moment when life is sparked, or at least that's what my conservative Southern sex education classes ingrained into me. Knowing that Alissa and I could never conceive naturally felt like another queer heartbreak. On the queer developmental milestones list, conception grief comes right after realizing you never slow danced with a girl in high school, but before the first time your son asks if Grandpa is his daddy.

"I've never had sperm inside of me!" my wife, Alissa, cheerfully announced to a room of medical staff in the middle of her first IUI procedure. Intrauterine insemination (IUI), commonly known as the turkey baster method, is a fertility treatment where a doctor calculates the exact moment you're likely to conceive. When the time comes, they insert a miniature garden hose into your uterus and pump you with semen. We laughed. The medical team smirked. Maybe they'd grown tired of gay infertility humor? On his way out, the doctor said, "Best of luck" and patted my shoulder in a way that made me feel oddly masculine.

With the combination of modern medicine and sheer luck, Alissa got pregnant after the second turkey basting. Nine months later, we had our son.

Our kid turned out to be such a joy that after his third birthday, we decided we'd try for another baby. This time, we decided, it would be me in the stirrups, my blood being taken, and my uterus being probed. The medical aspects of infertility made me queasy, but at least Alissa would be there distracting me with jokes or at least holding my hand.

On the morning of my own first fertility appointment, I stopped short at a jarring sign: *Partners must remain in the waiting room.* "Excuse me?" I said to the front desk lady. "Does that mean I have to get pregnant alone?" I pointed to the sign. "My wife and I are twice vaccinated and once boosted," I added, chewing the inside of my lip and thinking, surely, this sign couldn't be for us.

"Covid protocol states that your partner must remain in the waiting room," she said, keeping her eyes on her computer screen while her fingers never stop clacking. Her gum smacked. My chest contracted. I do not want to get pregnant alone, I thought. This appointment was for monitoring, but I knew that next time, I'd be here for the procedure.

The night before my first IUI, I decided to try making the best of it. "At least let's get lunch afterward," I suggest.

"Ok," Alissa says, "but I hate that I can't be in there with you." We lay 3 feet apart, not a toe touching. "It isn't fair; don't they know that being together is all we have?" I say, feeling sorry for myself.

In the gray waiting room, Alissa is working. Her fingers

tap incessantly between her keyboard and her phone. I am not working. I read *Eileen*, which is a story about a depressed woman who doesn't kill someone and then escapes her sh*tty hometown. The book makes me want to have a cold beer the same way reading *Girl on The Train* made me thirsty for gin and tonics. "Look at those fish chasing each other," Alissa says, pointing to the tank in the middle of the waiting room. "Those are Dory fish, like from *Finding Nemo*," I say. We go back to typing and reading.

The nurse calls my name and waves me back to the procedure room. A rose quartz crystal and a moonstone appear from Alissa's pocket. She dubbed these our fertility crystals when she was going through treatments. "Good luck," she says, kissing me and placing the warm stones in my palm.

Inside the exam room, I remove my underwear and jeans and fold them into a tidy square. These days, I merely trim my vagina hairs and I wonder what everyone else is doing with theirs. I am sure the doctor knows, but I promise myself that I won't ask.

Waiting, I lie down and place my socked feet in the stirrups. A familiar double tap knocks on the door and a smiling doctor and serious-faced nurse enter. They get straight to work opening instruments that sit in sealed bags and have me sign a piece of paper swearing that they have the correct vial of sperm.

"You're going to feel a small pinch," the doctor says as she inserts the speculum. I heave out a sigh, willing my body to relax. "Now I am going to insert the catheter into your uterus." I see the miniature garden hose. It looks longer than I remembered. Sweat rolls down my ribs. Looking up at the ceiling, I squeeze the crystals and take circular yoga breaths. "You doing alright?" the doctor asks. I wiggle my toes, loosening my muscles.

I let out another breath and realize my body is not in any pain. Unclenching my fists, I release the death grip on the crystals. The stones feel heavy in my hands, and I know I can handle this on my own. "OK, we're sending in the sperm," she says. I smile, realizing I haven't had sperm near me in more than a decade. When I start to feel settled, the procedure is over. She instructs to remain lying down for 10 minutes and reminds me not to be alarmed if I see light spotting.

The after care pamphlet reads: If you can, have sexual intercourse this evening. Allegedly, orgasms can help induce pregnancy. Since I have time to kill and I'm an overachiever, I decide to jerk off, twice. Sounds of the tissue paper blanket rustling back and forth fill the room. I text Alissa: I got myself off, twice. She texts me back: LOL

I wait 11 minutes before leaving. "How was it?" Alissa asks. "It was totally fine," I say and realize I'm feeling strangely confident and powerful.

We picnic on the Central Park lawn, eating sandwiches and chocolate chip cookies. I eat my entire Reuben and one-quarter of her veggie and cheese. I've never been hungrier. "It smells like dog piss down here," Alissa says, dipping her chips into my Russian dressing. Tiny birds bounce all around us, and I try shooing them away. "The park animals are too comfortable," I complain. Despite it being midday in July, it feels cool in the shade. I watch Alissa, who is watching a French family argue seemingly about directions. "I'm glad we did this," she says, gesturing to the picnic. Maybe it's the afternoon light or the fresh sperm or the excitement of possibility, but right this second, everything feels very romantic.

Alissa hails a cab to head back to work and I walk to the subway thinking about conception. The act of conception is not itself a precious act. It's clear that being in a room together for a medical procedure is not all Alissa and I have. What we have is a family and a city that has allowed us to live as openly as we've wanted. Queer people have long used creative interventions to build families. Queer people have helped build this island as a sanctuary to live outside of mundane and crushing cultural norms.

Alone, I sit on the subway, crystals in hand, and feel content, knowing I am now a part of this ever-expanding legacy.

# Other Mother

I felt like an *other mother* before my son was born. At the time, I diagnosed myself with a novel condition I called *belly envy*, a lesbian-specific complex in which one develops jealousy surrounding the pregnant partner. Symptoms included: feeling excluded, irritability, irrational urges (such as zipping off your wife's stomach and attaching it to yourself), and clinically significant levels of concern for your wife's physical safety. Most distressing were the preoccupations about my lack of shared molecules telling me I would be perceived by my newborn as a stranger.

When my son arrived my sense of other-motherness spiked. I felt frantic that he wouldn't know who I was. For his first weeks here on Earth, I wanted to hide our family of three on a faraway island, so we could bond without interference. Watching his genetically related family members hold him made me sick with envy.

We didn't leave our Brooklyn apartment for a life of solitude, though, and while I carried my otherness with me, soon I was submerged in soothing, bottle making, bottle scrubbing, and near constant awakeness, leaving me little time to think about it.

During this time, I developed a psychic ability to wake up 30 seconds before he started screaming in the night ready to eat. And it was me, not his DNA-compatible mother, that best quelled him when he experienced evening episodes of a kind of cry described by the Internet as "occurring just because." I understood that being alive is tough, so the idea of purple crying was not strange to me.

While the sense of other-motherness faded in relation to our growing, mutual attachment, fresh forms of otherness sprouted. I felt the novel *Monster Mother* one morning when my newly walking baby wouldn't stop tearing every book off our shelf. He was also screaming, happily, just practicing his lung capacity while heaving books. No shushing or distractions or *Cocomelon* video could stop him. I watched as the cover of Elie Wiesel's *Night* was torn in two. Before I could explain to my son that he had committed a hate crime, the thicker-than-a-Bible biography of Diane Arbus shot across the room and hit our tiny schnoodle. The clock read 6:40 AM. and, for a moment, I felt sure I would never make it through the day.

I survived that day, and the next, but I found myself spending more and more time fantasizing about solitude. There I was, sleeping in a cabin upstate deep in the forest, baking in an oversized kitchen somewhere lush and clean à la any Nancy Meyers film, and there I was sitting in a loud bar, guzzling cheap beer and flirting with the bartender as if I didn't have a life on a ninth floor apartment overlooking a school yard and church steeple.

At the playground feigning interest as other tired parents talked about sleep schedules and teething toys, I felt like an alien. They spoke like experts on en vogue child development (no, I still haven't read *Cribsheet*), and not only could I not keep up, but I didn't care. I wanted to gossip about Erika Jayne's legal woes or hypothesize about who the killer was in *Big Little Lies*. At the park, a half circle of moms stood holding babies while lunging. The more athletic ones held their babies out directly in front of them with straight arms. I strolled my son past, avoiding eye contact, radiating with secondhand embarrassment. I felt disconnected from mommy culture, and although I didn't want to be part of it, it was isolating.

It was during this spike of isolated motherhood that I interviewed Nina Renata Aaron about her memoir *Good Morning, Destroyer of Men's Souls*. Knowing she had also written the essay "On Why Middle-Class Parents Are Awful," I couldn't help but ask her about parenting. "Do you have *any* mom friends yet?" I asked bluntly.

She laughed and told me that eventually she was able to make mom friends who were more like her, "slightly more broken, honest, depressed, just people who are more real about how challenging it is. And those have tended to be moms who are single moms, people who make a living in nontraditional ways, people who've been through some stuff."[1] It was the first time my other-motherness connected me to another parent, and it was a salve. The obvious revealed: I wasn't the only parent contending with this novel, consuming identity. Swaths of parent misfits existed. After the interview, I felt motivated to lean into my complicated feelings about parenting. For the first time I could see a world where I could find connection with other parents and maybe that would tamper my sense of otherness.

Since talking to Aaron, I've been trying to pay more attention to all the other mothers in plain sight. In Chloe Caldwell's memoir, *The Red Zone*, she writes about how "being a stepmom has some undertones of what being queer feels like; they can both be invisible."[2] Writer and singer Allison Moorer writes of the isolation of being a parent to a nonspeaking autistic child in her book *I Dream He Talks to Me*. On a particularly difficult pandemic parenting day, I stumbled across the poem "Motherboard" by Kate Baer, and I've marathoned every available season of *Workin' Moms*. Every little bit helps. When chatting with other moms at school drop off or at play dates, many conversations revolve around feelings of being ill-equipped, antecedent of parenting mistakes, and the sharing the nagging sense that we are irrevocably fucking up our children in one way or another. It seems most moms feel, in some sense, like an other mother. There is a clear assumption from moms that everyone else is doing it better. As I collect stories of other mothers, I feel less alone and more connected to the identity.

My son is now 3. He is cautious and hilarious like my wife. They have identical chins and matching dark brown eyes. He is concernedly stubborn and stops to sniff flowers and examine sidewalk bugs like me. While he is not molecularly mine, he is clearly of me. Most days, I feel securely attached, and I'm starting to become more confident in who I am as a parent. Occasionally other-motherness rears, but it no longer feels as visceral - or as threatening.

I'm trying to embrace all the mothers inside of me instead of reading them as a sign of inadequacy. Through media consumption and conversations with parents the more I see we're all struggling; *who am I now? Am I doing this right? What am I doing that my child will talk about in therapy later? Why do other parents look like they know what they're doing?* The balloon of otherness and solitude deflates replaced with the clarity of knowing that a sense of otherness is the most universal parenting feeling of all.

# How Horny are Moms?

An examination of mothers and their
relationship to their sexuality

Statistical analysis calculated and
reported by Jordan Freeman

## Abstract

**Objectives**: Society has long found it impossible to view women as independent sexual beings. This inability to view women as autonomously sexual only further deteriorates with the onslaught of motherhood. Motherhood is a time when women are further devalued as singular people and more intensely viewed as a construct and an object belonging to something or someone else, i.e. children, spouse, and society at large.

Cultural references to mothers and their sexuality are extreme; we have examples of the frigid, under-sexualized mother and as her counterpart, we have the chaotically horny mother (this mother tends to be also be correlated to craziness and out of control behaviors - a specific notion to conflate robust sexuality with insanity, but we'll save that deep dive for another day). Many of the modern assumptions surrounding mothers and their sexuality lie within the historical Madonna-Whore complex. According to the website, *Modern Intimacy*, "The Madonna Whore Complex (MWC) is a psychological complex often perpetuated by heterosexual, cisgender males which places women into two categories the Madonna, a woman who is pure, virtuous, and nurturing, or a Whore, a woman who is deemed as overly sexual, manipulating, and promiscuous. The dichotomy of MWC creates a rigidity that limits women's sexual expression, agency, and freedom by defining their sexuality into one of two categories."[1] In our modern society where women continue to be viewed primarily within the context of others (children, spouse, parents, siblings, etc.) it makes it difficult to recognize women, mothers or not, and their relationship to their sexuality as a trait solely of their own.

This study will examine if mother versus non-mothers have differing relationships to their sexuality, and determine once and for all: how horny are moms?

Hypothesis: The researcher hypothesizes that mothers and non-mothers will score similarly across measures of horniness (frequency of partnered sex, frequency of masturbation, self-identified relationship to their sexuality, etc.) thus showing that mothers are women, and women are people, and people have their own independent relationship to sexuality that is complex and varied. No difference between the mothering and non-mothering group is hypothesized to exist.

Materials and Methods: A self-administered questionnaire was completed by 135 participants. Volunteers were garnered via Instagram and were not awarded any compensation for their participation. The questionnaire contained choice answers and some fill in the blank open-ended responses. We collected 135 unique survey responses, where 82 respondents were mothers (61%), and 53 respondents were non-mothers (39%). Statistical significance was determined by Jordan Freeman, MPH.

Conclusion: Overall, there was no statistically significant difference in "sexuality" between mothers and non-mothers. In other words, mothers compared to non-mothers show no significant difference in levels of horniness, meaning both mothers and non mothers have individual, complex relationships to their sexuality.

So, then how horny are moms? It totally depends on the mom!

## Introduction

My first vivid introduction to considering mothers as sexual beings occurred in the year 2000 when I watched the film *American Beauty* alone during a sleepover at 4:00 in the morning. As per usual, all the other girls were sleeping, but as the token gay (despite not knowing it at the time), I remained wide awake due to the nervous energy my body felt from being in a group of 12-year-old girls who seemed to understand what exactly that meant.

In *American Beauty*, actor and American icon, Annette Bening plays an ambitious and "frigid" wife (often ambitious women are associated with being "frigid"- another curious idea to look into at a later time. I use the word "frigid" here as that is how her role is described in numerous online sources). In the film Carolyn's (Annette Bening) husband Lester (Kevin Spacey*), is supposed to be the film's protagonist and the character we empathize with, although even as a tween this felt off-kilter. Lester is in lust with his daughter's best friend, which we are supposed to believe is totally kosher since she's 18. We watch this grown adult man daydream about her in sexually explicit ways and then we see him almost have sex with her, before finding out she is a virgin, which was even a bridge too far for the old creep.

*I KNOW- yuck!

In the movie, Carolyn develops a crush on her slightly older colleague. Carolyn and the colleague have an affair, which ultimately helps Carolyn feel like she is coming back to life after years of living the unfulfilled suburban dream. Within weeks, Lester discovers the affair and punishes Carolyn for her behavior, by berating her and essentially telling her that he is going to start living life however he wants without consideration for her (as if he hadn't been doing that already).[2] The message was clear; men are allotted endless room for their sexual desire and fantasies, while mothers' desires should remain for their husbands, and punishment should be swift and harsh for attempts at fulfilling alternative sexual desires.

*American Beauty* opened me up to the ways outside forces attempt to control women's sexuality and how easy it is to internalize these messages. After this film, I began recognizing other archetypes of mothers in relation to their sexuality. Namely, Stifler's Mom in *American Pie* who presents as wildly horny and unhinged.* Then there was *Unfaithful* where we see a mother's sexuality provoke her husband to commit murder. Richard Gere's character is so offended by his wife's affair that the only way to assuage his ego is to literally murder the man. Finally, I think of the Todd Haynes film, *Far From Heaven*, which follows the dissolution of a 1950s housewife, Cathy and her husband Frank. In the film, we discover Frank is a closeted gay man. We see him on screen engaging in homosexual

---

*The character's name is Jeanine Stifler, which I had to look up since in my mind she is merely *Stifler's Mom*. It feels like there is something to be said here about never having memorized the horniest character by her actual name. Worse, that we collectively refer to her by her son's first name.

behavior while Cathy's parallel story line is her forming a deep friendship with the black gardner, Raymond.[3] This friendship is shocking for the racially segregated town. The takeaway being that gay sex is just as radical as a cross-racial friendship in this fictional 1950s town? It never felt right to me that Cathy doesn't have a full affair with Raymond or at least passionately kiss him at the end of the film as he boards a train leaving town. Frank is out there having a full sexual awakening, while Cathy is what? making a good friend? Justice for Cathy and Raymond! Give this woman a sexual awakening of her own. Why wouldn't Cathy have an obvious inkling of sexual desire for this handsome man who is empathetic and understanding of her life? All of these films are examples of wide ranging stereotypes which have taught us that mothers have extreme disinterest or obsession with sex, mothers who are highly sexual are wild/crazy/ill/adulterous, and further that it is reasonable to punish women for their sexuality.

In 2014 writer and director Simon Stone updated the classic play *Medea* starring Rose Byrne and Bobby Cannavale. In the updated version, Anna still kills herself and her children to spite her estranged husband at the end, but in this version he has said the quiet part out loud and deems her no longer desirable after she has given up her body and career to mother their children. He has an affair, which he initially gaslights her about, but then owns up to, although blames her for his behavior and justifies his actions. Before committing filicide and dying by suicide, Anna delivers a gut wrenching  monologue that deftly explores ideas we've previously discussed about mothers:

You thrived on me, you grew, you blossomed, and I slowly died. You took my career away from me. After all those nights, all those years of sleepless nights of solving your problems for you, and all those nights you were too tired to fuck me even though I'd done all the work, and all of the day of pretending to be at work while you pretended to be a scientist, and all of it I had to put up with because I thought at least he needs me, and he knows he needs me, and even though he doesn't fuck me anymore, at least he'd never fuck anyone else.[4]

In some ways, we have progressed since I was 12 in our cultural ability to view women as independent people seeking their own sexual pleasure, but I would assert the most growth has been gained among single women. Let us not forget the horniest *Desperate Housewives* storyline, Gabrielle Solis (Eva Longoria) who had an affair with her too young neighbor, was the only childless woman on the Wisteria Lane. Notable progress has been made for childless characters in examples like Issa Rae's show *Insecure*; Kris Krauss's, *I Love Dick*, although the book was published in 1997, the show gave it a more public presence in 2016; Mae Martin's show, *Feel Good*; and the novels *Big Swiss (Jen Beagin)* and *Luster (Raven Leilani)*- to name a few.

Before collecting my own data, I attempted to review prior examinations of motherhood and sexuality. A recent 2021 study titled, "The impact of motherhood on sexuality" (Anna Fuchs, Iwona Czech, Agnieszka Dulska, Agnieszka Drosdzol-Cop) from the School of Health Science in

Katowice, Medical University of Silesia, Poland examined the quality of the sexual life of women throughout the first year of childbirth.[5] While I believe documenting and not just assuming is imperative for society, I had to laugh and scream out loud because the first-year postpartum is like living in altered version of reality where you live in varying haze and fugue states. This is further true for birthing parents who have had their body split open either naturally or with medical assistance. I didn't need to read the results to know that women don't have satisfactory relationships to their sexuality 1-year post partum. But I went ahead and read to confirm. Not shockingly, pregnancy and childbirth reduce female sexual activity and lack of desire. However, mothering lasts a lifetime, so again I am wondering what the relationship is between mothers and their sexuality.

I found a seemingly more interesting study from 2010, "Perceptions of Women's Sexuality Within the Context of Motherhood" by Shannon Trice-Black. Off the bat, this study notes that most of this research concerns early post partum moms. (LOL of course early post partum moms don't want to fuck! Save your research dollars.) This study lacks, in that the data hinges on a mere "five middle class women, ranging in ages from 35 to 40. All participants were Caucasian." This small exploration did highlight that first and foremost women need to be aware of their mental health, and that good mental health and care taking of oneself is positively related to satisfaction in sexual health. The results noted, "that many women sacrifice much of themselves for the needs of their children and their spouses. Along the way, the voice of the self is sometimes lost." And that, "much of the sexual focus is often on the pleasure of the man."[6] Now these are ideas we love to see in scientific writing!

Finally, a third study titled, "Sexuality and Motherhood: Mutually Exclusive in Perception of Women" from the journal *Sex Roles* by Ariella Friedman; Hana Weinberg; Ayala M Pines looked of particular interest, but was blocked by a firewall, so we'll never know their findings.

## Analysis*

**Study Sample**

A questionnaire was disseminated via a link on the author's public Instagram Story, asking mothers and non-mothers to volunteer for participation. Mothers and non-mothers interested in providing feedback filled out the survey; no compensation was provided. We collected 135 unique survey responses, where 82 respondents were mothers (61%), and 53 respondents were non-mothers (39%). Participants' ages ranged from 21-70 with a median age of 34 and an average of 37. Eighty-four percent of the sample reported being married, fifteen percent unmarried, and one percent unknown. Ninety-six percent of the group identified as women, four percent identified as nonbinary.** Eighty-nine percent of participants identified as white, one percent identified as black, and ten percent identified as non-black Hispanic and other. Fifty-eight percent identified

---

* Statistical analysis conducted and compiled by Jordan Freeman, MPH
**This author did not feel it necessary to have transwoman disclose in an alternative category

as heterosexual, thirty-nine percent identified as either homosexual, queer, bisexual, or pansexual. One percent identified as asexual.

## Methods
*For Questions 1-5, identified in "Results" section*

To determine the statistical significance of any measured difference between mothers and non-mothers, a chi-square test was conducted using an "alpha value" ($\alpha$) of 0.05, where a calculated "p-value" was compared to the alpha. Statistical significance was measured to determine whether the studied variable (sexuality) happened by chance, or because of a determining factor (motherhood). If the p-value measured greater than the alpha value (0.05), then we could not reject the null hypothesis, and there was no statistically significant difference between the compared groups (mothers and non-mothers). In this instance, we wanted the null hypothesis to stand (i.e. we wanted to show that there was no replicable difference in levels of sexuality between mothers and non-mothers).

Our Null Hypothesis was as follows:
*Null Hypothesis: There is no statistically significant difference between displays of sexuality between mothers and non-mothers.*

Compared to:
*Hypothesis: There is a statistically significant difference between displays of sexuality between mothers and non-mothers.*

*For Question 5, as identified in "Results" section:*
Responses around frequency of partnered sex and masturbation were collected as free text. To analyze this feedback collectively, responses were placed into 5 categories to mimic a Likert Scale measurement: Never (where responses to "Do you masturbate?" and "Do you have partnered sex?" were "No"; *Rarely* (less than 6 times per year, or where responses included things like "Rarely…," Depends…," "Irregularly…," etc.); *Sometimes* (once to three times per month); *Often* (once to three times per week); *Most Days/Daily* (four times per week or more).

*For Question 6, identified in "Results" section:*
To determine any correlation between negative body relationships and fewer instances of sex/masturbation, a Correlation Coefficient was calculated. If this calculation fell between 0.1 and 1.0, it would posit a positive correlation between the two variables (sex/masturbation increased when body positivity was present). If the calculation fell between -0.1 and -1.0, it would indicate a negative correlation (one variable decreasing while the other increased). If the calculation fell closer to zero than 0.1 or -0.1, then there would be no identified correlation. When reviewing the calculated Correlation Coefficient, we knew that numbers closer to 1.0 or -1.0 indicated a stronger correlation, whether positive or negative, while also remembering that correlation does not insinuate causation. Causation between these two variables (one *causing* the other) falls outside the scope of this study.

## Results

Overall, there was no statistically significant difference in "sexuality" between mothers and non-mothers. In other words, we determined that the measured differences in "sexuality" in this sample occurred by chance; if we were to collect another set of surveys, we should not expect the same results.

**1) Who self-reports to be hornier: moms or non-moms?**
In our sample, 48 mothers (59% of mothers) responded "Yes" to the prompt: "Would you describe yourself as horny?"; 28 non-mothers (54% of non-mothers) responded "Yes" to the same prompt. Though we observed a slight difference in mothers' and non-mothers' self-description of their horniness, we would almost certainly be unable to yield the same results from a different sample.

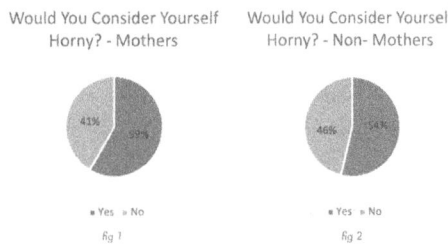

Would You Consider Yourself Horny? - Mothers

Would You Consider Yourself Horny? - Non- Mothers

41% 59%

46% 54%

▪ Yes ▫ No

▪ Yes ▫ No

fig 1

fig 2

**2. Is there a statistical difference between moms and non-moms for masturbating and having partnered sex (separately)?**
Any observed difference between mothers and non-mothers

on questions of masturbation and partnered sex in our sample were not statistically significant, though we did measure some difference between the groups.

89% of moms responded "Yes" to the prompt: "Do you Masturbate?" versus 94% of non-moms. Of the moms who reported masturbation, 62% masturbate often. Of non-moms who reported masturbation, 70% reported masturbating often. Overall, a higher percentage of non-moms said they masturbated and masturbated often.

For partnered sex, more moms reported having partnered sex than non-moms (95% of moms vs. 87% of non-moms). More than half of both mothers and non-mothers who reported having partnered sex are doing it often, at 55% and 57% respectively.

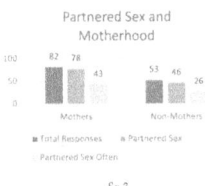

fig 3

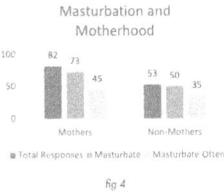

fig 4

# 3. Which group wishes they were having more partnered sex?

In our sample, mothers and non-mothers reported almost identical desire for more partnered sex; moms at 78% and non-moms at 79% responded "Yes" to the prompt: "Would you like to have more partnered sex?"

### 4. Which group has a more negative relationship with their body?

Again, any observed differences between moms and non-moms are not statistically significant or reliable (meaning, cannot be replicated in another sample). But, in our sample 32% of mothers responded "Negative" to the prompt "How would you describe your relationship to your body (Positive, Neutral, Negative)?" versus 34% of non-moms. A higher percentage of mothers responded "Neutral" (45%) than non-mothers (38%), and a higher percentage of non-mothers responded "Positive" (28%) than mothers (23%). In both groups, less than a third of responses were "Positive."

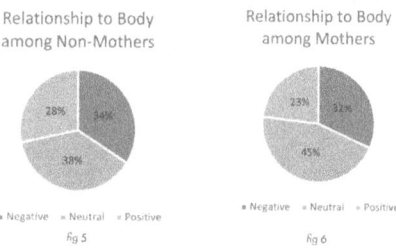

Relationship to Body among Non-Mothers

Relationship to Body among Mothers

■ Negative  ■ Neutral  ■ Positive

fig 5

fig 6

### 5. Which group is more likely to be VERY in tune with their sexuality?

When asked "What is your relationship to your own sexuality?" with possible responses "very in tune," "somewhat in tune," "not in tune," or "I don't think about it," moms responded "I am VERY in tune with my sexuality" 37% of the time, and non-mothers 40% of the time. But, these differences are not statistically significant.

### 6. Is there a relationship between negative body relationships and fewer instances of partnered sex/

**masturbation?**

Overall, any correlations observed were very weak. In our sample, there was a very weak positive correlation between a positive relationship with one's body and frequency of partnered sex for both moms and non-moms. (Correlation Coefficients of 0.15 and 0.19 respectively). When examining the frequency of masturbation and its relationship to a positive relationship with one's body, there was no correlation observed among non-mothers (-0.007). Among mothers, there was a weak negative correlation between masturbation and a positive relationship with one's body. This would indicate that as mothers garner a more positive relationship to their body and their sexuality, their frequency of masturbation decreases. You could hypothesize here that perhaps an increase in body positivity would inspire more partnered sex, and thus less masturbation? Though partnered sex doesn't necessarily negate masturbation? Just a theory….which we cannot confirm in any way.

## Discussion

Firstly, this study demonstrates no difference between the overall levels of horniness between moms and non-moms. To the initial question: How horny are moms? This study was able to demonstrate that the horniness of moms is completely individual and varies. You'd have to ask her. Interestingly, when reviewing results from optional fill in the blank sections on the survey, it was clear that moms compared to non-moms were more likely to fill in this section.

Fill in the blank follow-up questions: "Anything else you want to share about your relationship to your body?"; "Anything else you'd like to share about your personal sexuality in relation to having children or not having children?"

Particularly when answering the question, "Anything else you'd like to share about your personal sexuality in relation to having children or not having children?" moms wrote in complex, thoughtful, and surprising answers including the following, which are printed anonymously with permission:

> *My attachment to monogamy loosed somewhat after I was done having kids. I feel this is probably more common than acknowledged.*

> *I am a consensually non monogamous mother. My sex life is very important to me, and has become even more so after having a child. My spouse is very supportive of me finding time for myself to be sexual alone and with other people. We have a great relationship, and I'm very happy to be creating a positive example for our child of what healthy relationships can look like. I feel like I'm living my life as authentically as possible, and really loving this phase of my life.*

> *My partner is extremely balanced in helping with domestic chores and childcare. I absolutely would feel less interested in sex if he were more typical of male heterosexual partners in not sharing domestic and*

*household work equally. I feel very valued because our household responsibilities are so balanced, which leaves me feeling like having sex with him all the time.*

*I feel like having children has made it harder to have the time and energy for sex. I miss feeling horny. It also has negatively influenced my relationship with my body. My pelvic floor was also affected by the carrying and birth of my children, and despite lots of PT, sex doesn't feel the same.*

*I don't know if it changed much? The first year was tricky because of the nursing - I just wanted my body to not be serving others' needs all the time and that reduced my interest, but I'd say on the whole I feel more sexual. That may relate to my age/maturity and not my status as a mother.*

*Prior to kids and while pregnant I was very confident with my body and I was successful in my career. After baby I became a stay at home mom and I feel like I've lost myself a little bit cause I'm managing my 2 year old and my husband most days. And my body is definitely not what it used to be and it's just been hard to find motivation to lose weight/eat better.*

*I wish my sex drive was higher since having kids- it's so complex but I really feel like the main culprit is being the primary breadwinner (by choice) for our family, working long hours and just feeling so physically and emotionally fatigued by the time my partner and I have alone time.*

*It's different pre/post kids but I think post kids it's actually more comfortable/freeing in a weird way. The bond (for me anyways) feels stronger and that allows me to feel more free with my partner. I think kids are an easy excuse for people to not prioritize intimacy in a relationship but I think being committed (as a couple) to prioritizing that connection is important.*

*I had a realization that pregnancy was traumatic, and after becoming a mother (adopted first child, birth second child), I avoided sex or didn't feel comfortable with it as if my body were afraid to conceive again. Also, after my first child I went through a period of not knowing how to dress to be a "mom." It changed my identity and I didn't know how to present myself or feel sexy, as I'd no longer had permission. This had nothing to do with my husband, but how the community might view me.*

*I'm a very sexual person and involved in kink/ bdsm/nonmonogamy, of course on my own time which has nothing to do with my child's life or my parenting. I'm an adult woman with an adult sexuality that I have every right to express. Nobody judges fathers for being whole, horny people but everybody judges mothers for it. While simultaneously masturbating to "MILF" porn.*

If anything, it appears having a child makes many

women more contemplative and in tune with their relationship to their sexuality, which many cited due to dramatic changes experienced with their bodies, partners, and relationship to themselves. It makes sense that such an upheaval would force one to reconsider all parts of their lives that perhaps previously felt settled.

Although fewer childless women responded to the open ended questions, when they did they were equally articulate in sharing their thoughts about their experiences, desires, and difficulties. Most meaningful, they were able to discuss why being childless was the right choice for them and examine their relationship to their body. The following are printed anonymously with permission:

> *I choose not to have children for several reasons. Although my body is designed to be capable of childbirth and pregnancy, I don't want to physically or mentally go through that. I do not want to have to be concerned about another human's life over my own, for the rest of my life. I'm happy and fulfilled, and I know that having children can bring happiness and fulfillment, but it would take away from what are my priorities and important to me now.*

> *I feel bad about my body and then feel bad that I feel bad about my body because I consider myself a feminist.*

> *Without children, it feels easier to fulfill any sexual desires as they may arise rather than scheduling it or waiting until a certain day/time, which can be helpful*

*given mental health difficulties that impact my sex drive greatly.*

*I grew up Catholic and you don't talk about sex, and I'm kind of uncomfortable talking about it and seeing myself as a sexual being. Honestly, I prefer to have sex with the lights off because I don't want to see myself at all. It makes me really self conscious.*

*Aging and body changes have impacted how I feel during sex and I don't always have a positive feeling about my weight but overall positive relationship with my body.*

*No desire to have children despite sexuality, not wanting to have children as a lesbian can sometimes create misconceptions about lesbian motherhood. I did not want children prior to coming to terms with my sexuality.*

These handful of responses from both mothers and non-mothers alone show the individuality and complexity of the topic. I can see many of their answers as potentially more interesting characters and plot lines than the one-dimensional versions of women we have discussed above. This study shows unquestionably, giving women the space to describe their experiences and thoughts is the best way to gain insight. It is my hope we continue not only creating spaces for women to speak freely about their complex personal lives, but when we do we are able to listen and form new ideas when it is required. Archetypes such as the frigid mom or crazy mom might make for easily digestible narratives, but they are shallow and inaccurate. Relying on outdated models lacks human nuance, which is what makes beautiful and interesting people/stories/lives/ etc.

Overall, this study nullifies one dimensional depictions of mothers and their relationship to their sexuality.

# Part IV:
# Womanhood

# Amends

"The violence I had orchestrated left my insides lacking…"

The *violence* I had orchestrated.

I had *orchestrated* violence.

*Had* I orchestrated violence?

I was prepping for a podcast, scanning through my essay collection, *Putting Out: Essays on Otherness*, when I passed by this sentence. I used to love it. When I read it, I could envision myself as a conductor keeping in time the crumbling of my early womanhood. I'd visualize the rotation of shot glasses, kegs, faceless men, loose pills, and strobe lights blinking in the basement bangers all circling around me like a halo. By putting myself on the conductor's podium, I could pick and choose what parts of my experiences I illuminated to others.

When I originally wrote the essay, titled "The Marine," I believed from the tops of my toenails to the bottom of my split ends that I alone had incited a man's violent actions against me.

Now, when I read the sentence, it feels like I am trying to stare at the sun. I guess you could call this revelation growth, but it's unsettling to know I lived in a haze of self-gaslighting. It feels further complicated knowing that if anyone, editors included, read this sentence, and questioned its validity I would have pushed back. Personal essay writing is seeking truths of one's personal past. It is a process highly limited by the beliefs and knowledge the writer holds in the moment of writing. I used to find irritation in reading my past thoughts and assessments, but now I see them as interesting moments to reconfigure and push forward. This story in particular encapsulates the struggle with my longest held belief: I am at fault for my assaults. Today my brain knows this to be untrue. I don't cognitively believe I evoked violence upon myself. The smartest part of me knows it was not my fault. I am still trying to convince my bones.

On her podcast, *Add to Cart*, SuChin Pak spoke about the 2021 Atlanta Spa shooting, where predominantly Asian American women were murdered. Pak, a media representative herself, called out the long and misguided language used by journalists to describe violence against women.

"Call it what it is, don't tell me the streets are dangerous. Tell me that men are killing women," Pak said to listeners.[1]

Pak urges the use of accuracy in reported language, and by doing so gives us a glimpse into how we've misheard accounts of violence for so long that it has stepped into our own psyches. From rereading my essay, it was clear from the misplacement of blame that it had steeped into mine.

My glaringly inaccurate sentence up for reexamination refers to an assault I experienced my junior year of college. I've never named it that before, *an assault*. In the past it was an *incident* or *that time when*. I want to use more accurate language when reexamining this story and insert the moments I previously omitted. Painstakingly, I crafted a story whereby leaving out portions I'd changed the impact, on paper anyway.

To amend a story of violence is terrifying. Rewriting takes away a perception of control that I need. There is also a risk of being fully seen or misunderstood by reexamination.

Writing about violence is difficult. To edit is human nature. In her essay, "Woven," Lidia Yuknavitch wrote, "In America, it's tricky to describe violence without it turning into entertainment."[2] I believe this is even more true when describing violence and women. Violence inflicted upon women is often *the* rising action in TV and movies, or *the* way in which to tie it all up at the end of a story. Women's bodies are used as literary vehicles.

To amend a story of violence is terrifying. Rewriting takes away a perception of control that I need. There is also a risk of being fully seen or misunderstood by reexamination.

What will happen if I stop editing this story? What happens if I am no longer *orchestrating*? What will happen if, like Pak urges, I *tell it like it is*?

The Marine: Reexamined

By the time I met him my stomach held at least four shots of vodka and likely two beers. I was no longer an ingénue freshman, but a well-oiled, self-destruction machine in my third year. No longer did I seek out guys for attempts at making emotional connections or to try to ignite a feeling of passion. ***It is only now looking back I can see*** ~~I knew~~ I was using them as a means to hurt, control, and occasionally feel good about myself. At the time, *I was acting on autopilot*.

About fifty of us crammed into a frat basement, which provided no relief from the summer heat that felt excessively stifling and damp, even by Virginia standards. He was enormous in a way that didn't typically interest me, with thick muscles pressing through a white T-shirt and standing a foot and some inches taller than me. *Which is to say, he was a cishet man and as a lesbian this was not a physicality that turned me on. This encounter, like the ones before, was not about desire. What is more depressing than separating sex from desire?* His body and demeanor rattled my insides with uncertainty though I knowingly targeted him. I walked towards him with no intent other than amplifying my initial feelings of discomfort. He spoke with an accent, or a slur, that I couldn't place and said he had been kicked out of the Marines.

The ex-Marine didn't attend our school but lived in our rural town and partied like a seasoned coed. My brain holds no formative recollection of our conversation.

As the evening continued, I fueled myself with more drinks and pushed myself toward him. At the time, fear felt more like an emotion worth chasing than a warning sign of physical or mental danger ahead. Regard for my well-being was essentially nonexistent, and I craved various forms of self-inflicted violence. *By crave, I meant I was living in a constant state of dysregulation, and I was relying on toxic coping mechanisms.*

Once acceptably intoxicated, *ie, numb*, I led him back to my apartment where we engaged in mundane sex. *At the time I thought my lack of excitement was related to the vanilla-ness of the act, but now I realize all sex without hunger is inevitably mundane. Per usual, I was checked out of my body.* When we met, I felt certain about his propensity towards violence and tried, with no avail, to nudge him to be rougher with me. Afterwards, I begrudgingly started to get dressed as he sat on the edge of my bed already tying his shoes. At least he doesn't want to stay, I thought.

We began exchanging the type of pleasantries that one gives after such a swift interaction when I said, "I've actually had better sex with women."

This sentence was a lie, although a hopeful one. The words bruised what I assume was his fragile idea of masculinity and before the last word left my mouth, he slammed me against the wall. ***The back of my skull bounced and vibrated against the drywall***. He held me in place with one hand- his middle finger to the bottom of his palm appeared to extend the length of my chest. My chest bone sank inward from the weight of his heavy hand.

*He pushed so hard that a cough escaped from my lungs.* I knew I had sensed an ominous presence in him. A moment later my body slammed back onto my bed as he hovered over me screaming ***"stupid bitch" and "fucking slut."***

I attempted to stand up and breeze past him, but he backed up, blocking the door. ***I peed a little and smelled the ammonia.*** While he continued to ~~rant~~ ***spew hatred at me***, I sent a S-O-S text to my friend who lived next door. By the grace of coming home last and being mostly blacked out, the front door was never locked, and my friend stormed in causing a racket and easily extricated him.

~~Although I located the disorder that I sought,~~ ***I didn't feel fuller after the experience. I did not get ready earlier that night with the intention of being brutalized.*** *Even if I had left the house with the intention of being physically brutalized by a strange man I did not control or create*

***the actions of the Marine.*** ~~The violence I had orchestrated~~ ~~left my insides lacking anything substantial and I realized~~ ~~I might be more numb than when the night began~~. My life had become a game of throwing emotionally charged darts at myself hoping one would stick. Back at my friend's house, the first memory I have is sitting on her kitchen floor surrounded by bubbly, drunken sorority girls eating pizza. The event wasn't discussed much further and I shoved it down as deep as I could, although this exercise was getting more difficult to accomplish as events were rapidly piling up.

Throughout the assault, I never acted as a puppeteer. Not once did I force his hands to grab my shirt, press his palm onto my chest, nor did I open his mouth and instruct him to spew hate in my face. And yet, I wrote of orchestration.

"I've had better sex with women."

***

For a long time, I told myself it was this speaking that caused him to lash out.

I am not sure why the use of my own voice has disoriented the events and led me to assume that I was the one to blame.

Instead of choosing simple, true words, I wove a tall tale. For over a decade I was content to believe my story.

My words did not cause violence. The rational, therapized parts of my brain know this, but even as a woman with a literal master's degree in psychology I did not always believe it. For years, I thought my skewed language was a means to keep me in control and feeling safe. I see now there is control in rewriting a fuller truth, albeit not as palatable.

# A Common Occurrence

*To not be raped* is nebulous…bodies amorphous…a common occurrence. It's a difficult location to pinpoint on the spectrum of violations. *To not be raped* puts the onus on the individual to detail their own experience. For me, it feels impossible to accurately describe the velocity, fear, and physical actions propelled onto my body over the years. Part of me feels like I don't want to.

OK, I'm lying, a little.

A big part of me feels like I could spend the rest of my life describing violence. I worry that I could talk about it every day for the rest of my life and still have more to say. This awareness pisses me off to no end. Should articulating these experiences be my life's work? Just because someone can, does that mean they have to, or should? I don't know the answer to this. Mostly I feel defiant - as if somehow by not illustrating the blow-by-blow, I win. I am not frightened to write from a position of vulnerability, but so often when we see violence against women, their bodies become an accessory, unattached, or a vehicle to move action along in the story.

In the summer of 2016, I experienced a not-rape. This particular not-rape felt like the pièce de résistance to my lengthy history of assaults. A few weeks after the not-rape, other past assaults, ones I had mostly left unresolved, somewhat festering, began cropping up in my mind. For most hours of the day, they were all I could think about. I thought I had boarded up my past securely with nails constructed out of overachieving, career milestones, drinking, and a light shellac of self-loathing were beginning to open. Coming loose was the past I packed away so tightly. I found myself Facebook stalking the boy, my origin of not-rape, from my childhood and staring at pictures of his ballooned-up face. His profile picture caused bile in my stomach to bubble, but I couldn't stop looking. His picture showed him wearing a camo jacket with neon orange outlines kneeling in a muddy field holding a deer carcass with a shotgun lying beside him. The smile on his face curled as if to say, *I deserve this*. My stomach turned and I examined his hands, which were much bigger now. It's probably hard for him to keep his past locked inside too, I thought. I always felt sure a sinister act had been committed against him, as that's not how well-adjusted boys behave. Although my stomach ached with disgust, I couldn't muster any anger toward him. Anger seemed impossible to conjure towards anyone other than myself.

My eyes burned, bloodshot from staring at the bright light of my phone in the dark room. No matter how long I looked at this grown man's face from my childhood, I couldn't accurately remember the other, more recent man. The inability to name and place this stranger made it feel more like a haunting. The floorboard of my past was beginning to rot and crumble, leaving me to try keeping my balance on the slippery surface of shame.

I felt embarrassed with my accumulated history of violations; Kevin in eighth grade who jammed his fingers inside me during a field trip bus ride, David the senior boy my freshman year of high school who tried ramming my head down on his dick when I thought we were going to listen to Dashboard Confessional and maybe kiss. I ran the mile and a half back to my house without stopping wearing Old Navy flip-flops while he logged online and told everyone at school that I blew him before I even got home. Ian, a frat guy in college who I actually did try to blow, but he had a bad case of whiskey dick. We laughed about it and shared a beer on the floor of my friend's bathroom. Two nights later he told his entire "brotherhood" at their Sunday night meeting that "Sam, that new Sigma Kappa girl, sucked my dick." The nameless Marine who threw me against a wall after we had sex and held me in place with his baseball mitt-sized hand while he called me a fucking slut. The other moments of gray and frequent times of *empty consent*, a term coined by Melissa Febos in her memoir, *Girlhood*, which she identifies as "affirmative consent given despite internal ambivalence, aversion, or revulsion."[1]

Looking at the list, it's easy to start believing that I must have been asking for some of it. I know - that's the thing I'm not supposed to say.

Despite our culture not having readily accessible language to describe this common occurrence, in 2018 Dr. Ford constructed her own experience of *not rape* for our country. Word by word she brought us into the moments she experienced with Supreme Court Justice Kavanaugh and his shithole friends. With each sentence formed, she illustrated to us the aftermath and the idiosyncratic ways in which she went on to live her life. After not being raped, Dr. Ford testified that she added an extra lock in her home, kept secrets with her therapist, and lived with an irrational, unshakeable fear that followed her no matter how she aged or has successful she appeared to the exterior world. She detailed an argument between herself and her husband about her need for a second door in their master bedroom. Dr. Ford couldn't relax in her own bedroom without multiple exit points.

I obsessively listened to Dr. Ford's testimony two years after my own not-rape during a time when I was struggling to put to words my experience and to understand shifting parts of myself. Dr. Ford highlighting her need to move her body, to always have a way to escape made perfect sense to me. I saw myself in her coping mechanisms and in her clear and steady, but still nervous energy. When questioned about what she remembered, Dr. Ford quickly stated, "the laughter. the uproarious laughter between the two and their having fun at my expense."This fact, and the strength of its memory being so accessible to her unwound something deeply composed in me and I began to sob. "I was underneath one of them while the two laughed," she continued. "Two friends having a really good time with one another."[2] Until listening to Dr. Ford, I had never cried about anything that had happened to me. Usually, I found anger and shame, but for a moment I felt wholly consumed with grief for Dr. Ford and for myself.

In her memoir *Blood*, Allison Moorer writes: "Awful thing upon awful thing piles up on people all the time… there isn't a calamity limit or bad luck quota."[3] On hard days, I try remembering that.

Fewer days are hard. Many of them are good. On one such good day I am making tomato and mayo sandwiches in the Berkshires on vacation with Alissa, our three month old, and my extended family. After lunch I managed to lull our unwilling baby to sleep, and send Alissa upstairs to take a nap of her own as I had slept in that morning.

The baby sleeps in the living room, tucked into an overpriced vibrating chair that rotates in him in various directions. Standing five feet away from him, I poked my head out of the sliding door in the living room looking out ahead at the shimmering lake. I was itching to get back into the water and steal away a few moments to myself. My father-in-law noticed my restless movements and shooed me to go on ahead, assuring me he'd keep an eye on the sleeping boy. Sliding open the door I stepped over my aunt-in-law, who was engrossed in *Cider House Rules*, a book she had read at least 10 times prior, but stated was a must for a summer reread considering the current political climate. Just months prior, Brett Kavanaugh had been sworn in as the newest Supreme Court justice.

"Hi sweetie, do you want to take the kayak out? Go! Enjoy the lake. I'll keep an ear open for the baby," she said, keeping her eyes on the pages. Under her umbrella-sized hat, she lounged in an oversized dog bed beside her massive geriatric dog, making sure they both kept themselves out of the scorching midday sun.

I walked down the uneven cement steps into the water feeling the smooth pebbles underneath my feet. The soft algae tickled my legs as I ventured out. It felt nice to be alone without needing to tend to anyone other than myself.

Warm water cut through my thighs, stomach, and chest. I tiptoed so far out the water hit my neck. When I could no longer stand, I pushed myself underneath listening to the silent roar of the world below. As I broke back up above the surface, I heard the audible gasp of my inhale. My feet no longer stood on solid ground. I swam out until I found myself in between our shoreline and the island in the morning. Looking out in all directions I felt far away; from the city, my past, and from the worst parts of myself. I managed to swim out to somewhere new. I allowed my head to bob, neither going completely below the water or all the way out above the lake. I hovered, appreciating the view from the space in-between. Like a fountain I spit out the brackish water and rubbed my eyes clear.

I felt whole and young, for the moment. Taking a deep breath, I resubmerged myself below, having nothing to sanctify or wash clean.

As I looked out across to the island in the middle of the lake, I imagined baptisms taking place at the shore. A tall man donning a white robe that floated and fanned out on top of the water dunked a fully clothed woman as he prayed aloud. She pops up out of the water, drenched and smiling, clearly feeling cleansed. All of us on shore belted out an Amen in unison. My twangy rumination ran loudly in between my ears as I viewed the entire scene drenched in my granny's bouncy accent.

Swimming back to the shore, I spotted the rest of my extended family in a clump of colorful floating inner tubes and paddle boards on the far east side of the lake. I'd known all of them since the pre-formed age of 19, so marriage and baby aside, they are my family. Their laughter bounced off the homes and trees. In the early afternoon, everyone was exactly where they were supposed to be. I sat on the dock soaking up their laughter, letting the sun warm my body, and reminding myself that forgiveness and healing are common occurrences too.

# You Told Me This Would Be Easy (on Abortion)

During a routine appointment at my fertility clinic, I found out I had miscarried. I had made it eight and a half weeks which, in the fertility world, is a celebrated milestone—the point at which a patient migrates from their fertility clinic to their regular OB/GYN. After four months of unsuccessful IUI procedures, an egg retrieval, and one round of IVF, I was eager to be on my way.

"I am so glad I won't ever have to come back here," I said to my wife over FaceTime as I sat swinging my legs on the exam table, waiting for the clinic's ultrasound technician to arrive. The second the words were out of my mouth, I regretted them. Within minutes of the exam, it was clear the fetus was no longer viable.

Shellshocked, with my wife still on FaceTime (COVID protocol prohibited partners from being in the exam room), I asked the doctor what my next steps would be, assuming he'd recommend taking a few months off before we tried again. He proceeded to give me three choices: 1) I could go home to see if I'd naturally self-abort, 2) take abortion pills, or 3) have a procedure called a Dilation and Curettage (D&C), a type of surgical abortion performed within the first fifteen weeks. I stared blankly. I had never thought about what needed to occur physically. I asked which choice would be the easiest. Without hesitation, my doctor told me that a D&C would be the smoothest route for my body. I scheduled the appointment for three days later.

I cried on the subway home, rage-ate a turkey sandwich (for the first two months in a pregnancy, cold cuts are generally not advised), and then pulled myself together. In many ways, I was lucky. I had a supportive network, outstanding health insurance, and I lived in a state that respected abortion rights. It wasn't lost on me that if I lived in Texas, or one of the other 13 states where abortion is banned, my doctor would have sent me home with condolences and the hope of an uncomplicated natural miscarriage. Natural miscarriages can be a gnarly, painful, and lengthy experience.

In her Netflix stand-up special, *Joke Show*, comedian Michelle Wolf describes how she had an abortion in the morning, popped a LaCroix, and then headed straight to work.[1] Of course, this is comedy, but Wolf isn't wrong when she asserts a narrative that presents abortion as routine and easy. Planned Parenthood has long advertised the statistic that 1 in 4 women will have an abortion by age 45 – a useful statistic for internalizing how commonplace the procedure is, but not one that makes much room for conversation about its occasional complications.[2]

On the day that I was scheduled for the D&C, my wife and I sat silently side by side in the waiting room of the fertility clinic. The usually lively space was quiet except for the sounds of the bubbling fish tank. It hadn't occurred to me that this clinic also provided abortions. I'd never wondered why all my attempts at procreation had been scheduled before noon, but now it was clear: termination procedures took place in the afternoon, and the office understandably wanted to keep these patients separate.

About five of us sat stoically waiting for the nurse to call our names. When it was my turn, I focused on each individual step: changing into a gown, putting on a hair net, getting the IV. I figured if I could handle each moment, then I could handle the overall experience.

No more than twenty minutes after I was put under, I awoke from anesthesia feeling as though my entire vagina, inside and out, had been bruised and beaten. The cramps swelled. I sipped on an apple juice and watched my blood pressure, thinking about Michelle Wolf heading off to the office. Was it possible she had—as so many do—deflected the reality of the pain in order to minimize it? Just a month prior, I had undergone an egg retrieval without general anesthesia, so I thought I had a grasp on post-surgical cramping. I was wrong. As my wife drove us home, I chewed nauseously on graham crackers, looking forward to lying down. For the rest of the weekend, I stayed in bed. If I didn't move, pain relievers mostly dulled the cramping. But any time I tried to walk it was a different story. After an unsuccessful Sunday stroll, I relegated myself to bed, where I stayed until Monday afternoon when I headed back to work.

Over a week passed before I could move around for extended periods of time without cramping, and it took longer for the bleeding and disconcerting blood clots to subside. The psychological side effects lasted longer: insomnia, mood swings oscillating between depression, rage, and elation. The insomnia has improved, but even now, months later, I have trouble falling and staying asleep. It's impossible to know if this is incontrovertibly linked with the D&C, but it is connected in my head—does anything else really matter?

As the mental and physical effects persisted, I began to wonder if my body was defective or if I was overly dramatic. I struggled to find personal anecdotes from other patients who didn't find their abortions to be as simple as a teeth cleaning. The only stories I encountered were associated with dangerous anti-abortion forces. I began getting pop-up advertisements asking me to donate to the National Right to Life (one of the most well-known anti-abortion organizations). Had we made an unspoken pact to downplay the occasional severity of abortion in order to protect abortion rights? Maybe we've deemed it necessary to stick to a straightforward narrative. I understand the desire, but where does that leave people like me, who believe abortion is utterly necessary and also experienced it as a serious procedure?

When I reached out to close friends who had undergone abortion procedures, each one of them related to my experience. Friends spoke of everything from depression to shame to surprising pain. Not one felt "back to normal" within one to two days. We all fell on a spectrum between PTSD and Michele Wolf, going back to work after her can of LaCroix.

The fact that my abortion was surprisingly difficult has not changed my thinking about its legality or necessity. Rather, I have come to believe that we've inadvertently fused the idea that a procedure which is routine for doctors is also always routine for patients. Technically, angioplasties, C-sections, stent procedures, and elective cosmetic procedures are considered routine for doctors, yet no one would expect any of those surgeries to be easy on the patient.

My sense is that my abortion would have felt easier if I had a more nuanced understanding of all the possibilities for how it would play out. If anything, this information might have decreased my anxiety and stopped me from obsessing about my physical feelings being atypical.

Before my own abortion, I was also under the impression that as a culture we'd made strides in normalizing the procedure. But when I confided in my friends, I learned for the first time that four of them had abortions within the last twelve months. Had they kept it to themselves—even in our liberal community, even within our friendship—partly because their experiences didn't match what is perceived as the norm?

My abortion was difficult. The recovery was long, and I'm not sure I'm fully healed in all senses. Part of me thinks even discussing this will cause people to perceive me as an anti-abortion traitor. Another part of me feels that, as someone who received excellent medical care, I have no right to gripe. Yet another part of me knows that many other people probably feel the same. I'm glad I had an abortion. Everyone should have the right to safely access one. And the experience was hard. And, we have to keep fighting for all of this to be true.

Taken from the comments section:

*I find a lot of this author['']s post a very selfish mindset. Discounting the evidence that she is not able to conceive to any nature* [sic] *extent to the point of fertilization, she mentions mourning the loss of potential life. It seems she's mourning what she can't have. Surely she could solve all issues by adopting a child. No need to worry about her body rejecting the baby, no need to worry about untimely pregnancies. Yet her solution is just to make the death of an unborn child, with intent or by convenience, normal.*

she is

mourning the loss of potential life.            she's mourning

.

. No need to worry about her

, no need to worry

# Standard Deviation

I wanted to be a woman who wanted to be pregnant, or at least could tolerate it. I wanted to be a woman who wasn't so difficult.

"Do you think the IUI didn't work because you didn't want it to?" my wife Alissa asks one afternoon, a week before my third IUI attempt. I have been on months' worth of hormones, and I'm chronically on edge, like someone going through withdrawal. I can't stand how my stretching skin feels. I never want to be touched. I am always looking for an argument. "Do you think I don't want to have this baby? Do you think I would be putting in all this effort if I didn't want a baby?" I yell. It's a shitty accusation, but she's right.

Alissa got pregnant after two unmedicated rounds of IUI. Her pregnancy was typical; hot, nauseous, and uncomfortable, but we were elated and felt closer than ever. Being the partner to a pregnant person came naturally-I was consumed with a drive to caretake and protect. At 39 weeks, she endured a traumatic 36-hour delivery involving an emergency C-section, a blood transfusion, and a 14-day stay in the NICU for our son. Our original plan was to take turns being pregnant, and after witnessing her survive and then struggle with post birth trauma, there was no question: The next one was on me.

Two weeks after my first round of IUI, I woke up cramping and bleeding, and I felt relieved. The loudness of my relief is confusing. I turned to Google: *relieved after an unsuccessful IUI*. Every article bounces back a variation on: *What To Do To Overcome The Pain Of Your First IUI Fail.*

I search Reddit, but still, nothing in the chats or message boards validate my feelings, just pages of extremely discouraged people in a lot of pain. If you can't find a shared experience on Reddit, I reason, then it probably doesn't exist. A week later I schedule my next monitoring appointment assuming that this round I'll feel differently.

Growing up I never dreamt of marriage or babies. I never pictured myself moon-round, rubbing my belly. For a long time, I thought this was due to my ambition, my disregard for living life in a way I viewed as stereotypical. But maybe I didn't fantasize about wedding cakes and soft-kneed infants crawling on kitchen floors because I never thought I'd find someone I'd want to build a life with. Eventually, I discovered that my wariness toward domesticity was an aversion to inequitable homes ruled by gender norms. Basically I didn't want to live in *A Doll's House*. Once I found a woman I wanted to spend my life with, my thoughts about marriage and motherhood changed.

I remember the first time I saw my shadow with a baby on my hip. It was the summer my son was 15 months old and we took a road trip to Long Island from Brooklyn. I stood with him in the parking lot of a wine and beer store in East Hampton as the sun was setting. Side to side I rocked him while watching my shadow move. I felt feminine and motherly. I didn't understand why getting pregnant or thoughts of being pregnant weren't making me feel the same way.

A week before my IVF procedure I obsessively google success rates, which hover around 55% for women my age. The percentage goes higher, around 67% the more often you have the procedure done. On the morning of the appointment, my nerves aren't a symptom of the potential for failure, but of the higher likelihood of success.

"Look," the doctor says. He points to a screen in the operating room. "Right here, the plushest spot of your uterus. This is where I am implanting the embryo." I wonder when my Valium cocktail will take hold as I watch a gray dot move along the screen before it is released. Legs strapped into stirrups, a tube reaching inside me, I think I should feel excited, or, at the very least, moved by seeing the possible creation of life.

At the Thanksgiving table, I try not to squirm as my aunt rubs my 8-week pregnant bump. I chew the inside of my cheek until I taste metal, to stop myself from telling her that despite the distention in my stomach, there is nothing in my womb. I don't say any of this out loud because the week prior an ultrasound technician shows me a heartbeat, and I haven't bled in over 45 days. Cognitively I know I'm pregnant, and yet I feel hollow.

The following week, a tech examines me and within moments her eyes drop to the floor, and she hurries out of the room to get the doctor. The doctor tells me the thing I already know: The fetus is not viable. On the subway ride home, I can't believe I am someone weeping openly in public. I feel like I dodged a bullet. But I'm overwhelmed with grief too. Because I know I can't pretend to want to do this again. And because it is a loss—of a child I very much wanted, just not inside me.

When I was a freshman in college and first started having sex, I didn't understand the mania. A friend would report details of her interactions, what she felt in her body and how having sex usually made her feel closer to the guy. Sometimes she would become so obsessed that the rest of us would say she'd been "dickmatized."

I didn't feel anything life changing. Even when I had an orgasm it felt surface level. If anything, it made me feel less emotionally connected. My friends encouraged me: *Guys don't know what they're doing-you have to tell them exactly what you like. Maybe you shouldn't have sex before you're in a relationship. Have you tried anal? Have you tried being on top? Have you been blindfolded? Did you ask for what you wanted?* It wasn't until I started hooking up with girls that I realized I wasn't sexually broken. It's easy to overpathologize your life when you haven't seen varied ways of being represented. I was never sexually defective, I was just a lesbian. I'm not maternally damaged, I just don't want to be pregnant. The truth isn't so severe.

The night of my abortion procedure I can't sleep. I wake Alissa and confess in the dark that I don't want to be pregnant -the whole experience never felt right. She apologizes for sensing it all along, but never making a safe space for me to openly disclose or for her to ask directly. She tells me that although she's nervous, she wants to carry our second child. It turns out, we were both hiding.

We now breezily joke that I ended a pregnancy with my mind. I mostly believe this to be true. I often think about others who feel similarly, but have less consideration for themselves and fewer options-not everyone has access to an extra uterus. I wonder what the unspeakable trauma of going through with it must look like. I've never seen it represented. What do you even call a woman who wants to be a mother but doesn't want to be pregnant? A gender traitor? A witch? It's as if a person who never wants to be pregnant isn't real. It often feels like when I reach for a word that doesn't exist it's as if it's designed to be that way.

The onus for coming up with language to describe varied ways of being has always been on the people who live it. Maybe the word for a woman who doesn't want to get pregnant, but still wants to be a mother, is my name. Or maybe it's yours?

# The Surprising Comforts of
*Dead Ringers*

In the first episode of *Dead Ringers*, which stars Rachel
Weisz as twin gynecologists, we see the two doctors deliver
various babies. A close-up reveals one twin using forceps
to pull a protruding baby out of a vagina, while the other
twin slices open a woman's uterus with precision, prying her
stomach skin back with forceps and extracting a baby from
the patient's body. Sounds of skin tearing, women laboring
in grunts and screams, and splatters of blood dripping from
vaginas and C-section lacerations echo throughout. At the
end of the scene, we are left examining an enormous gooey
pool of blood seeping over the hospital floor and staining
the doctors' white sneakers.

At the first touch of scalpel to stomach, I closed my
eyes, shielding myself from the carnage. But as I peeked
through my fingers, checking to see if the horror had passed,
it dawned on me that despite having a 4-year-old son, I had
never watched anyone give birth. During my wife's delivery,
I saw bodily substances I had never imagined: dirt-colored
amniotic fluid, pus, and a concerning amount of blood that,
just like on *Dead Ringers*, created a pool on the floor. While I
was by my wife's side for her emergency C-section, smelling
burning flesh and hearing the sloshing of suctioned fluids, I
remained on the other side of the sheet. I never actually *saw*
the main event.

How was it that I, a woman with extensive fertility
and pregnancy experience, hadn't witnessed childbirth

until it was presented to me on a fictional television series? Suddenly, I was concerned with how easy it had been for me to avoid. I rewound the first half of that *Dead Ringers* episode and watched the entire series wide-eyed. Then an odd shift occurred: The horror I'd thought I wanted to hide from started to feel like comfort.

*Dead Ringers* introduces the Mantle twins as representatives of competing ideologies. Beverly, the "Pollyanna" twin, wants to create a medical environment where people feel safe and supported in the process of childbirth. Elliot, the cynical one, is more interested in building a lab where she can figure out how to delay menopause (potentially forever), grow babies outside of wombs, and perform fertility experiments on willing participants.[1] Complicated ethical questions in this series are not resolved with simple answers. But the audience isn't left wondering if fertility, pregnancy, and birthing are gory and hardcore. And while *Dead Ringers* is certainly graphic, I did not find it disrespectful of people who have birthed or of their bodies. Rather, it is so authentically gruesome I have to wonder if watching this series may inspire people to feel empowered to take more agency over their own bodies in medical settings. And if medical professionals are watching, maybe they'll gain more empathy for their patients and begin viewing them as people rather than dollar signs.

As I watched the series, my own body and brain were finally starting to settle out from eight months of fertility treatments, which concluded in an eight-and-a-half-week pregnancy, a miscarriage, and a dilation-and-curettage procedure, a technical name for an abortion. Like Beverly, the twin trying to conceive through fertility treatments, I found myself curiously examining the blood clots dispelled from my body and was rattled by the lack of bodily control. Although our fertility processes differed, I was soothed by watching Genevieve, Beverly's love interest, assert with the conviction of a thousand dykes that she was going to impregnate her girlfriend. While not organically possible, she, like her lesbian foremothers, got it done - in their case, using an at-home sperm insemination. My fertility regimen was less intimate. It included three rounds of intrauterine insemination (IUI is the procedure where they "simply" shoot sperm into your uterus and hope for the best), an egg retrieval involving a barrage of hormone shots and daily pills, and a round of IVF, the one where they surgically place a fertilized egg into the plushest part of your uterus.

The entire process was unexpectedly painful for me - physically and mentally - but because none of the medical professionals around me said anything except "You're doing great" and "This might pinch," I assumed I was exaggerating my feelings.

The egg retrieval was particularly haunting. It was recommended to me that since I "tolerated IUI well" I should undergo the egg retrieval sans anesthesia. Looking back, I wonder what *tolerated well* meant. Maybe it meant I wasn't crying during the procedure, didn't wince too obviously, or said "I'm okay" when professionals asked how I was doing midway through their inserting a two-foot-long intrauterine-insemination catheter into my cervix and uterus. Had I seen what it looks like when a patient feels safe enough to ask for their needs to be met, the way some do on *Dead Ringers*, and for a doctor to be open enough to acknowledge that various pain-management avenues are available, maybe I would have thought more seriously about my options. Or maybe if I'd watched the procedure beforehand, I could have felt more prepared for how much it ended up hurting.

In the surgical room, I lay with my legs open and strapped into stirrups. A thin sheet spread across my lap acted as a vanity blanket. Everyone was in full surgical garb, monitors beeped, and yet I was wide awake. "This will pinch," the doctor said, thrusting a thin needle through my ovary. I audibly gasped. It was a punch-like puncture, nothing like a pinch. I panicked, knowing he would have to jab the needle through my second ovary. My heart monitor beeped faster. "Are you doing okay?" he asked - as if it mattered. He pushed the miniature vacuum around my ovary, sucking out eggs. Each time he pushed the vacuum to a new egg, I winced. He worked delicately and slowly, and I tried focusing on a constellation of green lights on the ceiling while practicing deep-breathing exercises. I looked at the clock. It had been approximately five minutes, and they estimated the procedure would take 20 in total. I did not want to be awake.

In retrospect, I'm reminded of another sequence from the first episode of *Dead Ringers*. A Black woman has just given birth, but after realizing there have been complications, her flustered husband asks for swift medical intervention from the nearest doctor. While not a medical professional, he knows something isn't right with his wife. Beverly, at the mercy of the busy New York hospital and all of its bureaucratic drama, tries to step in - only for another doctor to shoo her away. The woman eventually dies hours after giving birth, and all that remains are her bloody sheets. The hospital moves on, but the Mantle twins can't.

Watching someone ask a doctor for help only for their complaints to go largely ignored, while they're being made to feel like the situation was perfectly fine, felt eerily relatable to my own experience with fertility treatments and my wife's complicated delivery. As devastating as this scene and the everyday reality of it are, it was comforting to see the clear gaslighting and curtness of professionals played out onscreen. Often I have felt as if my questions about treatments and procedures have been brushed off - or worse, I've been made to feel as though I should just shut up and listen. The scene was uncomfortable yet validating.

*Dead Ringers* presents these dark moments as integral to understanding the current healthcare system and connects our present-day accepted horrors to the sordid history of the obstetrics-and-gynecology field. A character reminiscent of Dr. J. Marion Sims (the American "father of gynecology") is introduced, and the audience learns that, in the 19th century, he experimented on and tortured Black enslaved women without their permission, anesthesia, or painkillers. By the time the series introduced this historical information, I did not feel desensitized to the grisly details of childbirth and fertility treatments. Instead, I felt angry that I had no working knowledge of a field that so closely affected my life. I might not have constantly second-guessed myself if I had better understood the history of baked-in silencing and disregard for pain and bodily autonomy.

If I had known the brutal history of fertility treatments and the OB/GYN field, I likely would have felt more empowered to make a different decision about my own body. Watching *Dead Ringers* didn't change my medical history, but it did illuminate several harsh facts surrounding fertility, pregnancy, and birthing experiences that mainstream media have largely ignored. If I had known the truth, I might have asked for what I wanted and gotten what I deserved.

# Freud Killed Virginia Woolf

Depending on your vantage point, Sigmund Freud's legacy resides somewhere between the father of modern psychology and a misogynistic addict. As a professional in the field of psychology and a person who routinely benefits from mental health services, I can't wholly deny his additions to the field, including dream analysis and the structure of the psyche split into the id, ego, and superego. As a feminist and survivor of assault(s), however, my lens considers Freud from a more toxic and destructive angle. This destruction can be seen in his often-overlooked relationship with Virginia Woolf - a relationship that seemingly killed the depressed writer.

Everyone knows Woolf as the brilliant yet tortured writer who died by suicide at the age of 59. When others speak and write of Woolf, it's often made to sound as if taking her life was her destiny due to her history of severe depression and assumed manic episodes.[1] Frequently, she is discussed in a way that links her painful internal life with her work. People presume her suffering is what made her art so "brilliant." This is the word most observed when reading about her writing, and after a while it feels to me similar to the way people today laude female essayists for being "brave." It's a lazy and loaded compliment, in my opinion.

It's never been a popular notion that the creating, the writing, the making of something from nothing is and of itself what aided Woolf in managing her demons, and perhaps extending her life longer than we know. Woolf lives in our psyche as a morose figment of the Victorian era constructed by a century's worth of folklore and speculation. It has been less explored and underpraised how Woolf spent a great deal of her life trying to discern her psychology and origins of her pain in an attempt to heal.

In 1939 Woolf began a deep dive into her past experiences and family dynamics as a way to make sense of her life and construct an autobiography. She allowed herself to speak openly regarding her childhood abuse and gain insight into her early life by interviewing family and close friends. During this time, she began understanding that her childhood, which was saturated with violence, sexual abuse from her older half brothers, and almost complete emotional neglect from her parents likely contributed to her bouts of depression and "break downs."[2]

Physicians during this era believed depression, anxiety, and other mental difficulties were due to something being inherently wrong with a person, so Woolf spent her adolescent years being made to feel like a "bad" child from her own family and trusted doctors. In a letter dated November 26, 1906 to Violet Dickinson Woolf writes, "My life is a constant fight against Doctors follies, it seems to me."[3] As an adult Woolf distanced herself from these notions and began to see the important role her past played in her turbulent emotional life. Firstly, it is impressive to muster the internal trust to distance oneself from the parade of professional opinions she was bombarded with as a child and young adult. The ability to reject labels and characteristics of oneself given by others is no easy feat. Woolf's ability to do so highlights her strong constitution. With a new perspective she started to understand that her sadness and breakdowns were not due to a fault in her own psyche, but a manifestation of her upbringing. It's likely that being able to link her past with her history of depression and anxiety brought Woolf a sense of relief and allowed her to view herself as something other than a broken woman.

Up until 1897 Freud touted the female condition of "hysteria" (i.e. trauma/anxiety/depression) as a symptom of his then-famous seduction theory. Seduction theory states that mental difficulties arose in women who experienced early sexual abuse. Essentially, the theory matched Woolf's own intuitive ideas. However, Freud abandoned the seduction theory in 1923 and began heavily working with the idea of the Oedipus complex, which stated women reporting early childhood sexual abuse were most likely fantasizing about the instances. Furthermore, Freud's updated hypothesis asserted the women wished these events actually occurred, and it was this fantasizing that was neurotic and needed treatment.

It's unclear why Freud changed his theory so abruptly in such a dismissive manner. Some have speculated that Freud couldn't accept that seemingly respectable men in Victorian society were capable of the severity and breadth of sexual assaults they were being accused of by female patients. By changing his theory, Freud and other physicians at the time began actively denying women the ability to have their truth heard and adding confusion and suspicion to their lives. Victorian women, including Woolf, were being told not to trust their own memories and intuitions.

As Woolf fastened together the pieces of her life in the form of an autobiography she fell into a deep depression.

Spending time reliving and writing about her childhood was emotionally exhausting work. It couldn't have been easy for her to tackle her history and form intimate conclusions about her life with societal norms telling her that her perception of events were invalid and "medically" incorrect. It's not a stretch to assume this internal-external fight was maddening. It was during this time that Woolf turned to Freud, as many did of the time, and his writings sought comfort and understanding. Once Woolf started reading about drive theory her depressed state worsened and her sense of self faded. As Woolf scholar Louise DeSalvo wrote in *Virginia Woolf: The Impact Of Childhood Sexual Abuse On Her Life And Work*, "Reading Freud, in fact, urged her to abandon her own insights into the reasons for her depression and madness." DeSalvo added, "I believe that it eroded her sense of self. If she was right and Freud was wrong, she was not a madwoman, but a woman whose response to her childhood was appropriate, though painful. But if Freud was right and she was wrong, she was indeed a madwoman…"[4]

Virginia Woolf took her own life not long after a visit with Freud. While it shouldn't be neglected that Woolf and her husband Leonard were preoccupied with the possibility of Germany invading the UK, so much so that they made a suicide pact as a more sensible solution than being captured by Nazis.[5] However, suicide attempts and periods of debilitating depression plagued her long before the war. It's recorded during the last weeks of her life she was referring to herself as a "madwoman." This internalization of her struggles as a form of her identity (ie "madwoman") marks a drastic turn from Woolf's hopeful autobiographical work where she understands her hardships as a symptom of her difficult life, not a personality flaw. In this way, Freud's work can be directly linked to the death of Woolf. Just as she was making strides, he, one of the most highly lauded professionals of the time, traded in the comfort of his own psyche (the need to not view men as predatory monsters) to the lethal expense of his patients (putting the blame on his patients by outright denying their lived experiences of abuse and making them believe their abuse was a desired fantasy). The suicide rates for women significantly started to increase in 1923 when Freud disregarded his seduction theory through the 1940s when he began relying more on the Oedipus complex. Woolf and patients all utilizing Western constructs were now being made to believe, by trusted doctors, that their abuse did not occur and was worse than they wished it had. The original gaslight. A diagnostic tool to disorient a person from their truth. A heavy-handed blame.

Today early work in trauma recovery revolves around a patient making peace with the ways they survived. Many find their behaviors like eating disorders, self-harm, sexual behaviors, etc. shameful and have internalized these behaviors as personality traits. A first point of relief is the budding understanding of present behaviors and related to past experiences. The phrase "normal reaction to abnormal events" is spoken by trauma informed therapists daily.[6] This understanding in addition to having a story heard and validated are critical in recovery.

Freud stripped these vital pieces of healing from Woolf

and his patients. The echoes carry today. We no doubt hear the prescribed blame in the phrases, "she wanted it," and "she was asking for it." Reports from RAINN/Rape, Abuse and Incest National Network note that 15 of 16 face no legal repercussions.[7] The 2023 four-time Tony Award-nominated play, *Prima Facie*, demonstrated how legal systems are set up to put the onus on victims to prove. *Prima Facie*, translates to believing the first impression until proven otherwise. The entire premise being as upside for survivors today is as true as it was for Woolf. The first impression originated with women in Woolf's time as hysterical, delusional, attention seeking liars compared to the *prima facie* of women today as overly emotional, delusional, attention-seeking liars. Of course it is still impossible for us to #BelieveWomen.

Woolf died by suicide in 1941. Ultimately, we'll never understand the exact circumstances or reasons that led to this. However, it is not a radical conclusion to discern that a woman who spent her life in pursuit of revealing truths, be that of her own or human nature, found it unbearable to live with doubt. Despite not having a clear path forward, Woolf rejected the diagnoses and doctors of her youth and forged a theory of her own . To then have her theory dismissed by a giant of the time who replaced it with a broken sense of self is devastating. How many times should we expect a woman to articulately tell us her truth before we believe her? Or before she finally shuts up? Or before she stops trying? While we don't have to dismiss the entirety of Freud's contributions, we should continue to closely examine both sides of his legacy to better understand him, the era, and how these ideas impact our current culture.

# Is It Too Late for Us to Apologize to Katherine Heigl?

Is it too late for us to apologize to Katherine Heigl? Would she even forgive us?

Moreover, should she?

Like many people, my wife and I recently discovered *Firefly Lane*, a Netflix series based off the novel by Kristin Hannah. The series follows two women (played by Katherine Heigl and Sarah Chalke) as they navigate the traumas and dramas of their lives. It's funny, nostalgic, a little dark, and overall a positive reflection of female friendship. We loved it.

"Has Katherine Heigl always been this good of an actress?" I asked my wife halfway through episode one. Her portrayal of Tully, an overachieving, under-self-cared-for TV personality is spot on. It's difficult not to watch her when she is on-screen.

"She's always been great. Izzie Stevens was the best character in *Grey's Anatomy*! I haven't noticed her too much in the past few years, though," my wife said.

"Yeah, well, that's because she's a bitch and a nightmare to work with," I said immediately before gasping, unsure why those words spewed so easily from my mouth. My unconscious bias had come roaring out of me without pause. Despite being almost one year into a global pandemic, living in a near constant quarantine, and slogging through seasonal affective disorder, my scrambled brain was still able to recall that Katherine Heigl was one of America's most hated actresses.

While I like to think that I'm smarter than I was in 2007 when the rumors began circulating that Heigl was "difficult to work with," I've never since taken the time to examine their accuracy, or given her the benefit of the doubt. In a post #MeToo and #TimesUp world, I am now well aware that powerful industry men have been behaving badly since the dawn of time; since 2017, we've heard story after story about men behaving in dangerous and vile ways. I don't want to give a continued word count to these men or their actions – suffice to say, being labeled "difficult" didn't stop them from working or fans from flocking. All of this, however, was ripped from Heigl by mere rumors and a handful of unsavory quotes.

The "trouble" started for Heigl during a 2008 *Vanity Fair* interview. I put the word *trouble* in quotes because, examining the statement now, her words appear astute and perhaps progressive for the time. In any case, they were nothing that should have warranted trouble for her career or reputation.

When asked about her most recent film *Knocked Up*, Heigl said she found it "a little sexist." She continued, "It paints the women as shrews, as humorless and uptight, and it paints the men as lovable, goofy, fun-loving guys. It exaggerated the characters, and I had a hard time with it on some days."

She further explained, "I'm playing such a bitch; why is she being such a killjoy? Why is this how you're portraying women? Ninety-eight percent of the time, it was an amazing experience, but it was hard for me to love the movie."[1]

I've watched *Knocked Up* dozens of times, and from my perspective, this appears to be an accurate assessment regarding the character she portrayed in the film. In the same interview, Heigl also points to the antiquated idea of the shrew wife, the nag, all archetypes as old as time. These are ideas worth examining, and this interview could have started a much-needed conversation.

Film co-star Seth Rogen did not publicly respond until 2016 when, during an interview on Howard Stern's SiriusXM radio show, he stated he felt "somewhat betrayed" by Heigl. But Rogen then said, "I respect the fact that perhaps she realizes that [the interview] has hurt her career, and I don't want that to have happened to her at all, because I've said a thousand stupid things and I really like her."[2] If this is not a perfect example of gaslighting, I don't know what is: In this quote, Rogen perverts Heigl's correct observation of the film and her own feelings by boiling them all down to "stupid things." And while he shows us that men are given space to "say stupid things" without affecting their careers and reputations, he does not take the moment to highlight that this is an impossible double standard.

By 2016, Rogen had years to reflect on *Knocked Up*, Heigl's role, and Heigl's comments on the film. Why did no one ask Rogen why he continued to support the portrayal of a one-dimensional female character? I'm not frustrated that he stands by the film as a whole, but I do find it culturally stalling that he cannot appreciate and empathize with Heigl's point of view. This could have been an opportunity for Rogen to reflect on how to improve his craft. Everyone is allowed to evolve, if they choose.

While researching America's disdain for Heigl, I discovered an article from May 2014 LITERALLY titled "10 Reasons why Katherine Heigl is the most hated actress in Hollywood."[3] This article was the fourth listed article when I typed "Katherine Heigl difficult to work with" into Google. The reasons listed in the article are asinine, and I won't bother reporting them here, but I will tell you I cannot find a "reputable" news source that has a similar top 10 list for any man now claimed to be canceled; I even typed in "Matt Lauer."

In a January 2021 interview with the *Washington Post*, Heigl reflected on her reputation. "I may have said a couple of things you didn't like, but then that escalated to 'she's ungrateful,' then that escalated to 'she's difficult,' and that escalated to 'she's unprofessional,'" Heigl said. "What is your definition of difficult? Somebody with an opinion that you don't like?"[4]

Is it too late for us-the media, the fans, the industry-to apologize to Heigl? Apologize for not respecting the fact that she understood her worth, had a clear vision of what she wanted her career to look like, and (god forbid) was ambitious? I hope it's not. Let this be a time when we stop punishing women for having the same exact traits we work so hard to instill into little girls.

In her essay collection *Tomboyland*, author Melissa Faliveno writes about the idea of "tomboy taming," examining how society advocates young girls to embrace "masculine" traits when they are children.[5] Young girls are encouraged to be dirty, fast, capable, and confident. However, Faliveno points out, these traits are quickly trained out of girls with the arrival of puberty, at which point girls are pushed into more "feminine" ways of being. Almost overnight, these previously celebrated traits are discouraged and replaced with actions that are seen as more feminine, like caretaking, becoming physically demure, and above all, learning to be agreeable.

All of this leaves me to question, what do we really want for women? Because it sure seems like we want them to shut the fuck up once they become of age. It feels to me like we're punishing Heigl for not tomboy taming her instinct to speak up on her own behalf and believe in her talents.

Heigl ends the *Washington Post* interview with this quote: "I've grown into accepting that ambition is not a dirty word, and that it doesn't make me less of a feminine, loving, nurturing woman to be ambitious and have big dreams and big goals…It's easier to be happy because I have a little more gentleness for myself."

I hope we can all have a little gentleness for her, too. Even if we're over a decade late.

*In 2023 Ellen Pompeo (the star of *Grey's Anatomy*) sat down with former co-star Katherine Heigl as part of Variety's *Actors on Actors* series. During this interview Pompeo admits was right to call out the working conditions on the early days of the *Grey's Anatomy* set among calling out the sexism in Hollywood. "She was ahead of her time," Pompeo stated.[6]

# Sex is not a Substitute for Masturbating, DJ Khaled, and the Orgasm Gap

On the subway recently, while semi-purposefully eavesdropping, I overheard a woman telling her friend that she no longer needed her vibrator because she had a new boyfriend. Her friend laughed in agreement. I attempted not to make a judgmental face, lest I blow my cover. Not once did this woman mention that her new boyfriend was a rock star in the bedroom or that he was giving her the best orgasms of her life. She simply correlated having a boyfriend to the idea that she no longer *needed* to masturbate.

This sentiment wasn't novel; I had heard this exact sentence multiple times from various women throughout the past decade of my life, and the idea has always struck me as odd and archaic. A satisfying sex life with a partner is awesome and a base level of what people deserve in relationships. However, a relationship is not a substitute for masturbation. This is not an either/or situation.

People can have both. I'm unsure why so many women- and let's be real, cisgender women in relationships with men- believe they can only be giving themselves pleasure when no man is there to do it for them. Men certainly don't make declarative statements like this when they enter into relationships. Masturbating shouldn't be viewed as a consolation prize to a partner. Women deserve to have healthy and satisfying sex lives - no matter their relationship status.

By sheer luck, I've had the pleasure of spending my life surrounded by women who own their sexuality and eagerly share the most intimate details of their sex lives. In high school my best friends and I threw a holiday dinner party where we got dolled up, cooked our best homemade appetizers, snuck in a bottle of wine, and gifted each other the latest and greatest vibrators that our high school budgets could afford, which is to say no one received a Rabbit. I was lucky to have a group of friends who never associated masturbation with anything other than pleasure for pleasure's sake.

It wasn't until college that I realized this wasn't the norm. During this time, I had multiple women confide in me that they'd never masturbated, and for years I didn't believe them. However, it's been noted 89% of women reported masturbating, while 95% of men have reported masturbating. These uneven statistics give a clear picture of how women are made to feel about their sexuality.[1]

This shouldn't be surprising, seeing as we live in a culture that cultivates the idea that vaginas are inherently gross. The 2015 study in Great Britain also highlighted disparities among gender and oral sex while also providing a broader cultural understanding of why this occurs. The study was one of the first to show (which won't be groundbreaking news to any woman) that we are socialized to value men's sexual pleasure over women's, and that we're socialized to believe female genitalia is "gross" and "dirty."[2] Most notably, we've been sold Summer Eve's "washes" and douches, which have explicitly advertised the notion you can "fix" this gross/dirty vagina crisis. These products have been successfully mainstreamed despite the evidence proving douching can be harmful.[3] Your vagina is fine as-is; it's generally self-cleaning, like an oven, and only needs to be washed with soap and water. Sure, if it's hot outside and you've taken a spin class, it might not smell like…Summer's Eve Island Splash, but neither does your armpit. Humans are aromatic, living creatures-and Axe Body Spray hasn't created a line of products to keep men's musty, dick-cheese scent at bay. Men's genitalia don't smell like Island Splash after a spin class, either.

But the fear they are selling is working. In 2015, a study in Great Britain found that the majority of women have anxiety surrounding their partner's perceived reaction to their body, and the fear surrounding their own bodies led to a discrepancy in overall sexual enjoyment.[4]

Our lack of knowledge around female anatomy and sexual pleasure begins in the classroom. Only 13 states require sex education to be medically accurate, leaving the rest of the country to teach whatever is deemed best practice at their school. Pleasure, consent, and LGBTQ+ topics are often lacking in these curriculums.[5]

In the school of pop culture we have celebrities such as DJ Khaled saying he wouldn't give oral sex, despite believing a woman should be giving it. In a resurfaced 2015 interview with DJ Khaled on the morning radio show *The Breakfast Club* Khaled stated that he doesn't perform oral sex on women, but believes that it would be inappropriate for a woman to refuse oral sex to men - "It's different rules for men. You gotta understand, we the king." He goes on to reassure the listeners that he takes care of his women by bragging about the types of homes he has them living in and types of clothes he has them wearing. Khaled does not once mention the idea of giving a woman pleasure during sex as an indicator of taking care of her; he doesn't even mention that he provides any pleasure to women during sex. When directly asked if Khaled performs oral sex on women, he stated, "Never! I don't do that!"[6]

While DJ Khaled is the most recent man to make headlines for essentially declaring female sexual pleasure as optional, this idea isn't new. Women's sexual pleasure has been pushed aside for most of America's history.

America has made some progress in our public view of women. Generally, as a people, we now believe women are capable of working outside the home, we believe they deserve the right to vote, and we're starting to believe that women deserve to be paid as much as men for equal work. Our country cares about the wage gap, at least during televised conferences and in op-ed pieces. While you might be hard-pressed to find a man willing to go on record saying women deserve to make less money than men for the same job, men still seem comfortable believing women coming out of the same sexual experience sans orgasm is acceptable. We've managed to wrap our heads around the pay gap, but there is still a mental discrepancy with the orgasm gap. Modern sex is primarily a vehicle of pleasure, not procreation, so shouldn't everyone engaging in it come away with an orgasm, or at least a solid attempt at one?

Further, for many women, we've long been told that keeping a man sexually fulfilled is the best way to keep him around. Grandmothers, aunts, and older sisters have warned us that sexually dissatisfied men will wander. Furthermore, we've been conditioned to believe it's normal for men to feel justified cheating if women don't provide them with enough sex. Examining this combination of societal constructs and constraints, it's not surprising women don't feel as comfortable seeking pleasure for themselves. Society wants women to fear themselves; it's more profitable and ensures the patriarchy remains intact.

The same 2015 study also found women's fear of their own bodies have caused a discrepancy in how well they are able to enjoy oral sex compared to men. The women in the study felt "reluctant" and "shy" about receiving oral sex compared to their male counterparts, due to anxiety surrounding their partner's perceived reaction to their body.

It hasn't helped women that the fields of medicine and psychology have long devalued women's pleasure. Freud famously stated that clitoral orgasms were "adolescent," and as women mature, so should their orgasms (meaning that once women start having sex with men, they should orgasm through penetration).[7] However, in 2017 one of the most comprehensive studies about female orgasms was published in *The Journal of Sex and Marital Therapy*. The study found that a mere 18% of women could achieve orgasm through vaginal penetration alone. Almost half of women in the study reported that they need clitoral stimulation in order to achieve orgasm.[8]

The orgasm gap is real, and while making sure everyone is getting off is individually important, the cultural impact of the orgasm gap far exceeds the bedroom. Caring about women's sexual pleasure correlates to how we view women as equal human beings, and not merely as vessels for men's wants and needs. Valuing women's sexual pleasure means that, as a culture, we view them as humans who deserve equal treatment across all sectors of life. This translates into equal pay, appropriate workplace treatment, and a decrease in sexual violence and harassment towards women. While various reasons exist for sexual harassment and assault, one glaring factor is that women are viewed as sexual objects to men. Men need to stop feeling comfortable perceiving women as things that give and objects to take from. DJ Khaled's outdated ideas about men abiding by different rules than women are not only immature but perpetuate the dangerous idea that women and men shouldn't expect equality in sex, relationships, careers, or life.

Right now, sexual pleasure is still largely seen as for cisgender men. We center penetrative, heterosexual sex when we talk about and teach sex. To children, sex is defined as when a penis enters a vagina, as a means of reproduction, and we define the lack of having that experience as "virginity," regardless of any other sexual activity. And there are still people who believe the clitoral orgasm is a lie, or that women don't need or want sexual pleasure the same as men.

The women's movement wants equal pay, equal job opportunities, and access to safe healthcare. The fact is, masturbation is healthy and natural for everyone. It has a slew of positive side effects. It's been proven to relieve stress, help you sleep better, boost your mood and relieve muscle tension. It can literally make you a healthier, happier person.[9] But even if it didn't, the act of masturbating -

understanding one's sexual organs and being able to give oneself pleasure - is important on its own. The women's movement wants equal pay, equal job opportunities, and access to safe healthcare.

We often discuss equality in relation to things we can see and count, how much women make per dollar compared to men, the percentage of women who hold congressional and senate seats, the number of female CEOs, etc. While it's more difficult to quantify female sexual pleasure, it doesn't make it less important in the overall picture of equality. Women figuring out what they want sexually is just one of the ways for them to figure out what they want everywhere else in their life. By equalizing pleasure, women are prioritizing themselves.

I hope that woman on the subway learns that having a boyfriend doesn't mean she needs to stop masturbating. Masturbation is a way to help us equalize pleasure and allow women to focus on their wants and needs, outside of a relationship. Each aspect of our lives that we take ownership of and view as having value brings us one step closer to general equalization across all platforms. By leaving one out, we will continue to have inequality; all the pieces matter. No matter what, women deserve healthy and satisfying sexual lives. This does not have to include a partner.

# Redaction From a Former Flake

*Sorry, I can't make it. There's too much rain. It's too windy. I'm exhausted. I can't commute anymore today. #SELFCARE! I need to reschedule!* These are texts I sent endless times over the past five years as I've flaked out on friends, therapy appointments, and extracurricular activities.

"I'm an extremely low-maintenance friend," I tell any new acquaintance. By *low-maintenance* I mean: You only have to see me twice a year and you never have to return my texts, but please don't expect any more than that from my end. Schedules change, people are busy! Grow up!

The pandemic only fortified my impulse to cancel. Before I might have feigned an effort to reschedule, but post pandemic, I had no qualms about canceling at the last minute. The amount of money I've paid, happily, over the years for last minute therapy cancellations is enough to have taken my family on a European vacation.

Lately, however, I've been wondering for the first time if flaking is as beneficial to my overall mental health. I was tucked into bed watching reruns of *Nashville* and scrolling through my phone when I saw a picture of friends with silly smiles surrounded by drinks. I had flaked on this meetup, citing "lack of motivation," but what had I done instead? It dawned on me that these languishing feelings are most prominent when I cancel. "Taking care" of myself by staying home mostly leaves me feeling the same, if not slightly worse.

Then it hit me, like Cher Horowitz realizing she was in love with her stepbrother, what if self-care isn't doing exactly what I feel like in the moment? What might happen if I spent an entire month not canceling any plans? This included friend activities, medical appointments, and previously purchased tickets. (To give you an idea of my baseline: Earlier in the summer I attempted, on two different occasions, to visit *It's Pablo Matic* at the Brooklyn Museum, and despite buying tickets ahead of time and the museum being a 30-minute walk from my home, I didn't go either time.) Not canceling on my therapist would be tougher, as I'd spun the narrative that she likely loved getting paid to not have to work and that this was my contribution to women helping women. Finally, as part of the experiment, I forced myself to pay attention to how I felt after following through on each activity when my impulse was to cancel.

I am disturbed and disheartened to report that my mood improved and I felt more connected and more present every time I followed through. It took about a week before I hit my first hurdle, an overcast and rainy September afternoon. I was supposed to be meeting a friend for lunch in midtown, but it was dreary, wet, and I was in Brooklyn with a fully remote work day. Previously, any one of the above conditions would have been a valid excuse for me to flake, but I mustered on, strapping on a bra, swiping on mascara, and bravely leaving the apartment.

When I arrived, my friend explained she was having an overwhelming week and felt gloomy. She apologized for not being her usual upbeat self; I offered hot gossip and *Real Housewife* recaps in response, and left feeling energized by the encounter. Later in the week I had the urge to cancel on my therapist to make room for a nap, but I made it and for the first time opened up about my impulse to be a no-show. Halfway through the month, I began thinking of myself as Shonda Rhimes in her book, *Year of Yes*, where she spends the year forcing herself to go from introvert to socialite. If I could manage both biweekly therapy appointments then I couldn't imagine what could stop me.

Around week four I planned to attend a nonfiction reading series. At the last minute, I realized that I'd be sitting in the audience alone. The event didn't start until 7:30, which meant I would have to change from my house sweatpants into stiff jeans at the very end of the day. That night the sun set at 7:11, which only furthered my inclination to hole up. No one at the event was expecting me. It would have been the easiest flake of the month. But instead, I slipped on my Doc Martens and made it out into a cool October night just as the sun was setting into a stunning blazing orange. The backroom of the bar was hot and I instantly regretted wearing such a thick sweater. I didn't know anyone, so I was left awkwardly smiling at people with their friends. I accidentally drank three beers and left the event tipsier than I intended, but I ended up meeting an author I admire. On my walk back to the subway, I even tried an "experimental" hot dog from a very Brooklyn establishment, something that had been on my to-try list for years. The bun was soggy, the sauerkraut mild, the dog itself mediocre-but now I know! As I reached the subway, somewhat drunk but satisfied, I recalled the Virginia Woolf quote: "I will take my mind out of its iron cage and let it swim-this fine October."

Psychologist Caitlin MacCrate agrees that when trying to build new habits, setting yourself up to experiment with the new behavior within a specific time frame can be a good idea as it gives you a set opportunity to collect data. "Now you know how good it feels to not flake," she notes, "and it becomes much easier *by way of that experience*. You have substantive reason to not flake now, not just because of a moral imperative or abstract rationale." This is not to say that within this time period sticking to the newly desired behavior will be easy. Part of this, MacCrate explains that, "at a very basic level, we have competing desires. Sometimes those desires are difficult to weigh, clarify, and act on. Honest and meaningful self-inquiry to clarify what you want (and impediments to these aims) can help to outline the steps toward doing things that are good for you."[1]

Psychotherapist Danny Gellersen suggests thinking about what you want to accomplish as a whole, and allowing for some contradiction. "There probably were feelings of "I don't want to, I'm tired, etc." Making room for those feelings to coexist with your engaging the activity is in my opinion probably a part of what left you feeling so good *on the other side* of this experiment." To avoid acting on impulse he suggested taking things slower. "We don't always have access to motivation, and on those days it's more about sustaining the system/habit building than demanding something of yourself you don't feel."

As I neared the end of my non-cancellation month, feeling like my most superior self, I ditched a yoga class. "At least I made a donation to a community organization," I reasoned internally. Later, however, the low of not following through hit me, and I wondered why I had bailed. Gellersen reminds us that creating new ways of being takes time.

"Becoming a more reliable person can feel like a threat to our freedom-and in a way it *is* a threat to a degree of freedom. Don't panic if after this month you have slumps and want to return to flakiness! that would be understandable."[2]

I rescheduled for Friday knowing I could try again.

# Consider the Blood Moon

Three weeks before I was admitted to the psychiatric ER, I had a vision.

On a crosstown bus I stood squeezed between an elderly woman with an overflowing grocery bag and a boy wearing a worn school uniform with no sense of personal space. As the bus jerked along to Flushing, Queens, I focused on balancing so as to not squish the frail humans on either side of me. My elbow rested on top of the woman's bouquet of kale as I listened to a podcast interview with Margaret Cho. Traveling to my client's home via subway, bus, and by foot ate up a considerable amount of my day and the commuting was hell for my mind. The empty minutes often accumulated upwards to one hour of time where my brain had nothing active to focus on. Without stimulation my mind marinated in loops of remembering things I was trying to forget and trying to piece together events that didn't make sense.

Podcasts were a way to try to keep my brain focused and steady. At the time I didn't have the concentration to read or write. Every time I opened a book, I found myself staring out over the pages or rereading paragraphs multiple times realizing I wasn't retaining a word. Listening proved moderately successful at keeping the intrusive thoughts at bay. I listened as Margaret Cho explained how a few times each year she voluntarily checked herself into a psychiatric facility for a mental health tune-up.

As she spoke, a heavy weight dropped into my stomach, and I knew. It was not a voice in my ear or a moving picture in my mind, but a clear, loud knowing. The bones in my heels and split ends of my hair knew. I was going to the hospital, soon. I would wear double-sided gripper socks and an ill-fitted gown. I would be scared and alone. Although you can't cover your ears to silence your mind, I tried anyway. *Shut up*, I audibly whispered to myself. Neither the woman nor the boy looked up at me, which was one of a million reasons I loved New York. *Shut up* I repeated to myself a little louder while turning up my headphones to their maximum volume attempting to drown out the knowing. But it was too late. I knew.

Before I was hospitalized, I was busy running. I began forcing myself to journey up and down the bridges connecting Brooklyn and Manhattan around four to six miles. Running felt like it should be in my genes. Both of my parents could jog a 10K like it was a warm up. For me, the act felt labored, but it was better that I wasn't good, it hurt more, and I wanted to experience every second of it. As I ran, I pictured the violence leaking out of my worn shoes, seeping out onto the ground for some other passerby to scoop up into the soles of their own sneakers. I thought the hurting of my tendons and muscles meant *it* was leaving my body. After the completion of each run, I hoped I returned home with less.

"Please stay, go run later." Alissa pleaded with me every weekend morning as I sprung out of bed and laced up my shoes, heading for the door. Before the assault, it was a standing joke that Alissa and I mirrored the grandparents from *Charlie and the Chocolate Factory*. Our bodies, especially on weekends, spent the majority of time glued side by side in bed. We were ladies of comfort and leisure; taking meals and calls and watching the world pass by from our memory foam haven. Now, the violence rattling inside of me demanded my attention.

"I'll be quick," I said, lacing up my shoes and heading out.

My weak ankles stung, and my knees felt like they might blow out as the Williamsburg Bridge inclined. It's notoriously steep - most amateur runners give themselves the incline to walk. It was a Saturday morning and I didn't want to go, but my body couldn't relax in bed.

The view of DUMBO inched into my view as I huffed up the Williamsburg Bridge. The neighborhood moved in a scenic manner; families strewn in the grass below wielding ice cream cones of every color, children buoyed on the Carousel and sailboats breezed down the Hudson. Pairs of friends strolled past me making plans for brunch.

A towering, chain-link fence barred the pedestrians on the bridge from accessing the sky above and water below. Intrusive thoughts invaded my mind, eliciting images of my body crashing into the East River with a hard *smack*. I didn't actively want to die, but my mind was tired. The idea of *not being* was soothing to my churning brain and uncomfortable body; both needed a break. Less than 10 feet away, the M train thundered by crossing through the middle of the bridge, vibrating the bones in my toes and heels. Another high chain-link fence separated my body and the train's incredible force. Images flashed of my body slipping in front of the train's movement and smashing everything away. A droplet of sweat rolled onto my lip, striking my taste buds with brine. The taste jolted me back to the present: the aching of my feet and to the noises of the people bustling along the bridge. I thought about childhood vacations and running at Myrtle Beach in the early morning with my mom. "Keep your eyes on an object in the near distance and once you get there pick another spot. Before you know it, we'll have reached the pier," my mom instructed as we chugged along the shoreline. I heaved along the bridge anticipating upcoming markers, "Williamsburg Bridge Sign, Delancey Street, traffic signal, broken down Burger King, Katz," I whispered to myself.

No matter the number of miles I ran, I couldn't distance myself from it.

Before I was hospitalized I dreaded night. Sleep rarely came and when it did, it came in short, hot bursts. I'd bolt awake, damp, smelling like coins and ammonia.

Shouts of a Mariachi radio station blasted through our closed window. It was past 10 PM and the late-night cacophony became a sort of manic sound machine Alissa and I learned to sleep through. The sounds echoed loudest and most often in the current late summer months. When standing outside the apartment, Alissa and I never could locate the origin of the sound. If she didn't bear witness to the noise, I would have thought it was a phantom fiesta.

Alissa faced towards the window, away from me, setting all six of her phone alarms. Even though she didn't need to get up until six, her alarms started at 4:30 AM and rang 20 minutes apart, and up until this point in our relationship, I had never heard even one of them. In the past month bouts of insomnia kept me awake and it seemed as if the first alarm would ring just as my body was finally drifting into

REM. Clean soap emanated from Alissa's showered hair, and I let the fresh, familiar scent calm me. With a steady concentration, she switched the alarms on and off twice more as the final step in her nighttime ritual. An unwelcome desire to be touched spread through me. I wanted Alissa to roll over, wind her hand in between my legs, and tell me I felt warm and wet. My body wanted her to take a fistful of hair at my scalp and tug. I needed to feel her teeth scrape against my lips and jawline.

After her final check, Alissa plugged her phone in and rolled over. She planted a plain, dry kiss on my mouth before nuzzling into my chest and wrapping her arms around me. My insides stirred and the beat of the Mariachi band reverberated the walls.

"Do you need anything?" Alissa asked. "Maybe you should sleep in the nook tonight." she said, referencing the corner of our bed that had been pushed up against the window and wall. This arrangement was the only position our queen-sized bed fit into the pint-sized room. The shelfed window overlooked a picturesque Brooklyn backyard with vines crawling up a brick wall, draped café lights, and a table seating that looked like it was uprooted from a hip farm-to-table restaurant. Once a week I peeked out below to our neighbor's dinner party where hipsters held wine glasses drenched with condensation. Bright vegetables and rustic meats filled family-style platters along the table. Summer in the city was a time when most living things were thriving.

The nook felt safe, like being back in a crib. Alissa favored the spot, but in recent weeks began extending the location due to my heightening evening anxiety, sweat producing nightmares, and general lack of sleep.

"Maybe it will help, thanks," I said, getting up and walking the short 100 feet across our filmy hardwood floors to retrieve a Melatonin from the bathroom. Our apartment had so few square feet that I didn't need to switch on any lights to see as I walked through the living space, "kitchen," and then the bathroom. My lips pursed as I chewed the purple Melatonin tablet. Its grapey taste reminded me of sick childhood days tucked under a blanket watching cartoons while slipping in and out of naps. The pill's texture caused my nose to wrinkle and I pushed hard to swallow the fragmented pieces.

We tried to have sex, a few times, after the assault. We touched each other like pieces of expensive stemware and I never came. Thoughts of his overbearing weight and faceless frame occupied my mind. I never knew what images floated through her brain when I touched her, but I never asked. After a handful of awkward attempts, I declared a 30-day sanction to my body. Alissa didn't protest this temporary boycott. I didn't want to want sex, but the urge occasionally crept up provoking me.

The following morning, I watched half-awake as an orange glow soaked through the curtains. My eyes tracked Alissa flouncing through the apartment and listened to the familiar shuffle of her morning routine. The refrigerator opened and closed, the water in the sink ran, and the wicker basket holding socks and underwear scraped against the wooden shelf. A creak of the medicine cabinet opening, followed by two spritzes and then the creak of the cabinet closing. I smelled her, Jo Malone Wild Bluebell, a musky floral, before I saw her. She reached over me, unplugged her phone, and kissed the top of my head. The oversized metal door slammed heavy, and then the apartment was silent. Daybreak hadn't relieved my body of the pestering. I touched myself attempting to rid myself of the nagging sensation that lingered and as a means to soothe myself back to sleep. I touched myself fantasizing about the faceless man with an inescapable weight and pictured a more sinister ending than the one I avoided. I came twice. I finally felt tired, and my body was heavy. I was drained from not sleeping and crushed that these faceless fantasies were the sole images that could get me off.

"I want to leave," I pleaded to the head nurse. "Please let me check myself out."

"I can give you another Xanax or you can go find somewhere to lie down," she said, her eyes on the computer screen. I hovered. After a few more moments of typing, she hustled me down the unit floor into an open room, handed me a pile of thin sheets she referred to as blankets, and clicked on the television without leaving the remote.

It was November 2018, and I was in the emergency psychiatric unit at a Brooklyn hospital after a night of binge-drinking and uncontrolled wailing on myself. I had a history of cutting, but that had always been methodical, controlled, and secret. This was lawless; I punched my legs and bit any skin I could bring to my mouth. I had never acted so reckless. At a loss, my wife, Alissa, called 911.

In less than ten minutes, four EMTs stormed our small living room to take me to the hospital as I was deemed a danger to myself. I spat and screamed and thrashed as two of them carried me down a flight of stairs and loaded me into the ambulance. On the ride over I sat handcuffed, kicking the gurney in front of me. "Quit kicking," the EMT yelled. I kicked harder. My wife kept her hand on my knee for the whole ride. At 29, I felt simultaneously like I was 4 years old and 100.

I didn't know it yet, but what began as the worst night of my life was actually the beginning of something better.

I had spent the past 14 years dabbling in therapy. Since puberty I'd lived with varying degrees of depression and self-hatred due to childhood sexual abuse, which was later compounded by assaults I experienced as a young adult and the shame of hiding my sexuality. Growing up in a conservative Southern town, I didn't want anyone to know I was a lesbian who'd been abused. Being one of two Jews in my high school had been tough enough. I hated myself for hiding just as much as I hated my identities. Pretending all the time was suffocating work, so I managed by binge-drinking, sleeping with guys I loathed, and using box cutters to slice through my skin. Sometimes I took muscle relaxers during the day. But even with this constant internal distress, I presented myself as a chronic overachiever: I had a 3.9 GPA, partook in too many extracurriculars, taught Sunday school, earned advanced degrees, and always volunteered to work extra hours at the special-education school where I worked as a teacher. I thought I had my shit together.

When I arrived at the hospital, a doctor took my vitals and a nurse drew my blood. For the first time, I felt like I had been caught. The mayhem that I worked so hard to keep tucked inside was now being quantified by medical professionals. Everyone could see the crazy on me.

My irritability rose. My fist punched my thigh, and my teeth gnawed my shoulder. "I'm so hot," I yelled, trying to take off my top. Within seconds the nurse shot a tranquilizer into my arm, and just before I lost consciousness, I realized I was far past the point of pretending to be someone well.

I wasn't well; I was a woman who needed help and had for a long time. Drifting into a sedation, it seemed obvious that accepting support couldn't be worse than this. At about 11 P.M., I was awoken and transferred from the ER to the regular psychiatric unit for the remainder of the night.

After the nurse refused to let me check out, I curled up on the metal bench in the empty hospital room she'd taken me to, wondering if I could sleep. The hard metal against my back felt identical to the bench I laid on the night during my freshman year of college when I was hauled off to the city's jail for being drunk and disorderly. The austerity of the room and the isolation were the same too. But everything else was different. I was no longer an 18-year-old closeted coed. I was almost 30 with an established career and loving marriage. I had an entire life to lose.

Down the hall a woman let out a blood-curdling scream, and I watched a man with his hands deep inside his pants walk laps around the unit. I didn't want to see where I would be in another ten years if I kept living the same way. I wanted to learn how to take care of myself. I wanted to find an honest version of getting better. Laying in my wrinkled yellow gown and matching gripper socks, I smelled the alcohol and sweat seeping from my skin and knew I would never feign wellness again. This revelation was an enormous relief.

Just as I glimpsed optimism, a familiar voice startled me. I glanced up at the TV, dumbfounded to see home-chef extraordinaire Ina Garten. I watched as the Barefoot Contessa stood inside her pristine Hamptons kitchen quartering a pile of limes for Dark Rum Southsides. She advised I use fresh-squeezed lime juice, but of course store-bought would be fine.

My relief melted into embarrassment. I couldn't have Ina Garten here, in a place so bleak and déclassé; I wasn't even wearing a bra. Ina finished off the cocktail by stirring it with a long metal spoon. The spoon clanked against the glass in a familiar and, above all, civilized way. The shame of the hospital was brought into full focus as Ina's friends toasted one another among the hydrangeas and wicker furniture. I closed my eyes. I didn't want to face that world. I didn't want to be seen as insane or out of control. I'd been telling myself that once I was out I'd keep getting help, but seeing Ina - and by extension, the outside world - I realized how difficult that was going to be.

At exactly 8 AM Alissa returned. I waited to be analyzed, and God willing, released by the doctors. "Are you okay?" she asked. Her clothes had changed and her hair looked washed. "No, but I think I'm ready to be better," I said. She held my hand and kissed my shoulder. I hoped she believed me.

After being released from the hospital, I began earnestly treating my mental health. I didn't drink for eight months and then slowly reestablished a new relationship to alcohol, which worked for me. I started telling my family and close friends when I was feeling depressed or irritable or anxious, which was an enormous leap for someone who had previously always been "great." I took up a sincere yoga practice. I said things like, "I feel overwhelmed" and "I can't go out tonight because I'm worried I'll drink too much. Can we take a walk instead?"

During one such walk, my astrologically inclined friend and I strolled across the Williamsburg Bridge. Since I had confided in her about the hospitalization, she had been buying me amethyst crystals, swearing they possessed healing properties. I wasn't sure about the rocks' restorative power, but I was moved by her sentiment.

On our walk, she told me that on the night of my hospitalization there had been a blood moon.

"So what?" I asked.

"A blood moon ushers in destruction and rebirth. Now you're safe and can rebuild your life," she said in a tone too rosy for me, although her words felt true. My long-held fear of rejection for letting others see the worst parts of me had been proven wrong. Being honest allowed her and others to see me clearly and accept me fully. When I told a few friends and family about my hospitalization, they only wanted to offer support.

In the five years since I was hospitalized, I've learned the art of being still - of doing nothing - when I feel triggered or overwhelmed or anxious. I feel the awfulness, and sometimes I even tell someone else about it. Of course, there have been moments when I want to drink an entire six-pack or romanticize about how good it would feel to cut myself one more time, but I don't. I've leaned into the mundane practices of caretaking: therapy, even when I don't feel like it, saying feelings out loud, breathing, walking, and meeting myself with kindness.

As I trudge toward self-acceptance, I still feel the twinge of shame reflecting on being hospitalized, even though I know I would voluntarily check myself in again. I wouldn't have the life I have now without that night. I wouldn't have my marriage and the son my wife and I had together four years ago. I remind myself that there's nothing embarrassing about being a person who needs help. Whenever I've confided my hospitalization to someone there is a moment of obvious sadness from them when they realize what I'd been through. I've realized it's this sadness reflected back to me that I hate facing, although it comes from love. For me, learning to sit with sadness and move through it has been important, and a skill I couldn't have learned without letting myself connect to others during these sensitive exchanges.

In March, my wife and our son took our annual pilgrimage to Miami. While it always feels reviving to be in the sun, this trip felt particularly needed. In December, I experienced a miscarriage and D&C, which sent me into a familiar dark mental space.

Old intrusive thoughts appeared. They tried to tell me that my retired ways of being, like lying about feeling bad and turning inward, were the fix. But as tempting as some of the thoughts were, I knew now they were myths. They were simply shitty coping mechanisms that had kept me feeling shitty. I didn't spend one second during my miscarriage acting like I had it all together. Within days I texted and called close friends and family members, even friends who hadn't known I was pregnant. Letting people in diffused some of the heaviness. I let myself feel grief. I cried in public. I cried with Alissa. I cried in front of my kid, assuring him there was nothing wrong with being sad. I didn't hide how vulnerable I was, and it helped.

One night in Miami, we had dinner outside at a popular South Beach restaurant. We were watching people buzz by on the boardwalk - women selling cigars, the inevitable shirtless rollerblader - when I noticed the moon hanging low, oversized, and glowing bright red. "A blood moon!" I yelled, grabbing my son's hand. "Let's go look!" He cackled as we ran across the main throughway to the beach. I popped him up on a stone wall. "Blood moons are really special," I said, as we stood studying the sky while I reflected on how I'd evolved since my hospitalization.

I viewed every day like a blood moon, an opportunity for destruction and rebirth - now understanding both were necessary. Even though I was feeling a low-grade depression, I was also feeling young and whole. All of it was true, and more important, I knew it wasn't crystals or magic that got me to this new way of being. It was me who pushed myself to understand that life won't always feel all good or all bad. It mostly exists in the complex places in between.

# Notes

## Author's Note

1. Dicou, Natalie. "How I Learned to Stop Worrying and Love Being a 'Super Dyke.' *The Atlantic*, February 19, 2014. https://www.theatlantic.com/national/archive/2014/02/how-i-learned-to-stop-worrying-and-love-being-a-super-dyke/283931/

2. Mills, Olivia, Bates, County of Greene Virginia, Oxford University Press, and Julia Penelope. "What's in a Word: The Disaccord of Dykes." *Medium*, June 6, 2018. https://edspace.american.edu/atrium/wp-content/uploads/sites/1901/2022/06/Mills-2022.pdf.

3. Author Instagram survey, early 2024.

## Part I: Body Work
### Dismantle

1. Davidson, H. R. Ellis. "The Legend of Lady Godiva." Folklore 80, no. 2 (June 1, 1969): 107–21. https://doi.org/10.1080/0015587x.1969.9716624.

2. Tuch, Richard Howard. "Unravelling the Riddle of Exhibitionism: A Lesson in the Power Tactics of Perverse Interpersonal Relationships." The International Journal of Psychoanalysis 89, no. 1 (February 1, 2008): 143–60. https://doi.org/10.1111/j.1745-8315.2007.00006.x.

3. Thomas, Andrew George, Bridie Stone, Paul Bennett, Steve Stewart-Williams, and Leif Edward Ottesen Kennair. "Sex Differences in Voyeuristic and Exhibitionistic Interests: Exploring the Mediating Roles of Sociosexuality and Sexual Compulsivity From an Evolutionary Perspective." Archives of Sexual Behavior 50, no. 5 (July 1, 2021): 2151–62. https://doi.org/10.1007/s10508-021-01991-0.

4. Bosworth, Patricia. *Diane Arbus: A Biography.* National Geographic Books, 2006.

## The Looking Glass Complex

1. Desalvo, Louise. *Virginia Woolf: The Impact of Childhood Sexual Abuse on Her Life and Work*. Beacon Press, 1989.

## Good and Clean and Fine

1. Consumer Reports. "Is Bias Keeping Female, Minority Patients From Getting Proper Care for Their Pain?" Washington Post, July 29, 2019. https://www.washingtonpost.com/health/is-bias-keeping-female-minority-patients-from-getting-proper-care-for-their-pain/2019/07/26/9d1b3a78-a810-11e9-9214-246e594de5d5_story.html.

## Part II: Girlhood
### An Unlikely Shero (On How Jawbreaker Helped Me Get My First Kiss)

1. *Jawbreaker*. TriStar Pictures, 1999.

## Part III: Motherhood
### Other Mother

1. 1. Mann, Samantha. "Nina Renata Aron Wants You to Know That It Gets Better: BUST Interview - BUST." BUST (blog), February 26, 2021. https://bust.com/nina-renata-aron-destroyer-of-mens-souls-interview/.

2. Caldwell, Chloe. *The Red Zone*: A Love Story. Soft Skull Press, 2022.

### How Horny Are Moms?

1. Brownlee, Brooke. "The Psychology of the Madonna Whore Complex." Modern Intimacy, August 11, 2022. https://www.modernintimacy.com/the-psychology-of-the-madonna-whore-complex/#:~:text=The%20Madonna%20Whore%20Complex%20.

2. *American Beauty*. DreamWorks Pictures, 1999.

3. *Far From Heaven*. Focus Features, 2002.

4. Stone, Simon (Writer-Director). (2020, January 30). Medea. Live performance at Brooklyn Academy of Music Harvey Theater.

5. Fuchs, Anna, Iwona Czech, Agnieszka Dulska, and Agnieszka Drosdzol-Cop. "The Impact of Motherhood on Sexuality." Ginekologia Polska 92, no. 1 (January 29, 2021): 1–6. https://doi.org/10.5603/gp.a2020.0162.

6. Trice-Black, Shannon. "Perceptions of Women's Sexuality Within the Context of Motherhood." The Family Journal 18, no. 2 (March 9, 2010): 154–62. https://doi.org/10.1177/1066480710364130.

## Part IV: Womanhood
### Amends

1. Spotify. "Asian Hate & Gaslighting in Georgia," March 18, 2021. https://open.spotify.com/episode/6Y3w966xM1e h3Blz1dlhzv?go=1&sp_cid=f83912c636c95818f93e7fc9ae6 28c67&utm_source=embed_player_p&utm_medium=deskt op&nd=1&dlsi=90d9c46df47149e0.

2. Yuknavitch, Lidia. "Woven." Guernica, November 18, 2016. https://www.guernicamag.com/woven/.

### A Common Occurrence

1. Febos, Melissa. *Girlhood*. Bloomsbury Publishing, 2021.

2. Katz, A, Debra S. Katz, Lisa J. Banks, and Katz, Marshall & Banks. "Written Testimony of Dr. Christine Blasey Ford," September 26, 2018. https://www.judiciary.senate.gov/imo/ media/doc/09-27-18%20Ford%20Testimony.pdf.

3. Moorer, Allison. *Blood: A Memoir*. Da Capo Press, 2019.

### You Told Me This Would Be Easy (on Abortion)

1. Wolf, Michelle. "Joke Show." Netflix, 2019.

2. 2. Planned Parenthood. "1 IN 4 AMERICAN WOMEN WILL HAVE AN ABORTION BY AGE 45," February 19, 2018. https://www.plannedparenthood.org/planned-parenthood-pacific-southwest/blog/1-in-4-american-women-will-have-an-abortion-by-age-45.

### The Surprising Comforts of *Dead Ringers*

1. "Dead Ringers." Amazon Studios, 2023.

### Freud Killed Virginia Woolf

1. Dalsimer, Katherine. "Virginia Woolf (1882–1941)." American Journal of Psychiatry 161, no. 5 (May 1, 2004): 809. https://doi.org/10.1176/appi.ajp.161.5.809.

2. Barner, Kenidee and Portland State University. "Virginia Woolf and Freud : The Implications of His Work on Her Mental Health." PDXScholar, May 23, 2019. https://pdxscholar.library.pdx.edu/cgi/viewcontent.cgi?article=1837&context=honorstheses.

3. Trombley, Stephen and University of Nottingham. "Virginia Woolf and Her Doctors." University of Nottingham Thesis Dissertation, October 1980. https://eprints.nottingham.ac.uk/30895/1/290837.pdf.

4. Desalvo, Louise. Virginia *Woolf: The Impact of Childhood Sexual Abuse on Her Life and Work*. Beacon Press, 1989.

5. Barner, Kenidee and Portland State University. "Virginia Woolf and Freud : The Implications of His Work on Her Mental Health." PDXScholar, May 23, 2019. https://pdxscholar.library.pdx.edu/cgi/viewcontent.cgi?article=1837&context=honorstheses.

6. Kraybill, Odelya Gertel. "Trauma Survivors: Your Feelings Are a Normal Response to an Abnormal Situation." Expressive Trauma In (blog), January 14, 2019. https://www.eti.training/post/trauma-survivors-your-feelings-are-a-normal-response-to-an-abnormal-situation.

7. "National Sexual Assault Hotline: Confidential 24/7 Support | RAINN," n.d. https://rainn.org/resources.

## Is it too late to apologize to Katherine Heigl?

1. Fair, Vanity. "Vanity Fair, January 2008: Katherine Heigl Press Release." Vanity Fair, January 1, 2008. https://www.vanityfair.com/news/2000/01/katherine-heigl200801.

2. Staff, Thr. "Seth Rogen Talks Feeling "Betrayed" After Katherine Heigl'S 'Knocked up' Comments." The Hollywood Reporter, August 11, 2016. https://www.hollywoodreporter.com/news/general-news/seth-rogen-katherine-heigl-knocked-up-feud-918640/.

3. News24. "10 Reasons Why Katherine Heigl Is the Most Hated Actress in Hollywood," May 20, 2014. https://www.news24.com/You/Archive/10-reasons-why-katherine-heigl-is-the-most-hated-actress-in-hollywood-20170728.

4. Spencer, Ashley. "Katherine Heigl Is Done Apologizing." Washington Post, January 28, 2021. https://www.washingtonpost.com/arts-entertainment/2021/01/28/katherine-heigl-firefly-lane-profile/?arc404=true.

5. Faliveno, Melissa. *Tomboyland*: Essays. Topple, 2020.

6. Aurthur, Ramin SetoodehKate. "Ellen Pompeo and Katherine Heigl — Actors on Actors (Full Conversation)." Variety, June 6, 2023. https://variety.com/video/ellen-pompeo-katherine-heigl-actors-on-actors-full-conversation/.

## Sex is not a Substitute for Masturbating, DJ Khaled, and the Orgasm Gap

1. WebMD. "Your Guide to Masturbation," December 16, 2022. https://www.webmd.com/sex-relationships/masturbation-guide.

2. Sanoff, Rachel. "Stigma & Gender Norms Are Why

Many Straight Men Don't Go Down on Women." Bustle, April 12, 2016. https://www.bustle.com/articles/154093-stigma-gender-norms-are-why-many-straight-men-dont-go-down-on-women.

3. "Douching | Office on Women's Health," n.d. https://www.womenshealth.gov/a-z-topics/douching.

4. Sanoff, Rachel. "Stigma & Gender Norms Are Why Many Straight Men Don't Go Down on Women." Bustle, April 12, 2016. https://www.bustle.com/articles/154093-stigma-gender-norms-are-why-many-straight-men-dont-go-down-on-women.

5. USC Annenberg School - University of Southern California. "Online MS in Nursing | USC Suzanne Dworak-Peck." USC Suzanne Dworak-Peck School of Social Work, June 25, 2024. https://dworakpeck.online.usc.edu/msn/.

6. Kaplan, Ilana. "DJ Khaled Said He Does Not Perform Oral Sex on Women Because 'there Are Different Rules for Men' | the Independent." The Independent, May 7, 2018. https://www.independent.co.uk/arts-entertainment/music/news/dj-khaled-the-breakfast-club-oral-sex-interview-2015-a8337276.html.

7. Rao, Ankita, and Alley. "Fuck You, Freud: New Study Says Clitoral Orgasms Are Great." VICE, July 28, 2024. https://www.vice.com/en/article/fuck-you-freud-new-study-says-clitoral-orgasms-are-great-5886b7559848b145c38b4526/.

8. Oberhaus, Daniel, and Alley. "The Biggest-Ever Orgasm Study Tells Us More About How Women Come." VICE, July 28, 2024. https://www.vice.com/en/article/the-science-of-female-pleasure-still-needs-more-attention/.

9. Rd, Rachael Ajmera Ms. "Masturbation - How Does It Affect Your Health?" Healthline, May 6, 2022. https://www.healthline.com/health/masturbation-side-effects#benefits.

# Permissions

The following essays have been previously published. Slight editorial changes have been made to fit the tone for this collection and publisher style guide.

A version of "An Unlikely Shero (On How Jawbreaker Helped Me Get My First Kiss)" was previously published in *Isn't She Great: Writers on Women-Led Comedies from 9 to 5 to Booksmart* edited by Elizabeth Teets, first published January 16, 2024. Permission has been granted by the publisher, Read Furiously.

"The Keeping and Care of You" was originally featured in *Emrys Journal Online Volume 2* in July 1, 2020: https://medium.com/emrys-journal-online/emrys-journal-online-volume-2-4c27723edd5c.
Permission has been granted by the author.

A version of "Our Big Gay Jewish Christmas Tree" originally appeared on December 3, 2020 in *Kveller.com*: https://www.kveller.com/our-gay-jewish-christmas-tree-is-everything-the-holidays-should-be/. Permission has been granted by the publisher, 70 Faces Media.

"Southern Charm" was originally published on August 1, 2023 in ELLE.com: https://www.elle.com/life-love/sex-relationships/a44652578/sorority-sister-love-wife/. Permission has been granted by publisher, Hearst.

# Acknowledgments

Thank you to Samantha Atzeni and the team at Read Furiously for always trusting and supporting my vision. Thank you to my teachers and editors; Jessica Wilbanks, Jill Rothenberg, and Chloe Caldwell. Thank you to the writer girls, the most brilliant, hilarious, and relentless community of women who keep me afloat in the sea of "no's" and self-doubt. Thank you, mom and dad, for always encouraging me to keep writing. To Alissa, "thank you baby for giving me my life."

# About the Author

Samantha Mann is the author of *Putting Out: Essays on Otherness* and editor of the anthology *I Feel Love: Notes on Queer Joy*. Other publications include *Elle, Washington Post Magazine, Romper, Bustle, The Rumpus*, and others. Her work has been featured on *MisRepresentation, Cup of Jo*, and in Roxane Gay's newsleter *The Audacity*.

# Additional Books by Samantha Mann

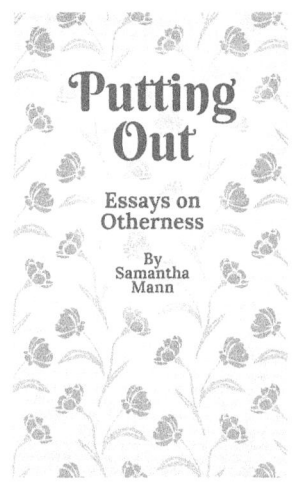

Learn more at
readfuriously.com/samantha-mann

# A Note to our Furious Readers

From all of us at Read Furiously, we hope you enjoyed our latest installment in our latest collection, *Dyke Delusions*.

Reading is more than a passive activity – it is the opportunity to play an active role to make our world better. We pledge to donate a portion of these book sales to causes that are special to Read Furiously. These causes are chosen with the intent to better the lives of others who are struggling to tell their own stories.

The causes we support encourage a sense of civic responsibility associated with the act of reading. Each cause has been researched thoroughly, discussed openly, and voted upon carefully by our team of Read Furiously editors.

To find out more about who, what, why, and where Read Furiously lends its support, please visit our website at readfuriously.com/our-causes

Happy reading and giving, Furious Readers!